CONCILIUM

concilium 1993/3

THE SPECTRE OF MASS DEATH

Edited by

David N. Power and
F. Kabasele Lumbala

SCM Press · London
Orbis Books · Maryknoll

Published by SCM Press Ltd, 26–30 Tottenham Road,
London N1 and by Orbis Books, Maryknoll, NY 10545

June 1993

ISBN: 0 334 03020 X (UK)
ISBN: 0 88344 871 8 (USA)

Typeset at The Spartan Press Ltd, Lymington, Hants
Printed by Mackays of Chatham, Kent

Concilium: Published February, April, June, August, October, December

Contents

Editorial   David N. Power and F. Kabasele Lumbala   vii

I · Burying the Dead in the Midst of Disaster   1
The Famine in Africa   3
  SIDBE SEMPORÉ
Burying the Victims of Natural Disasters in the Philippines   13
  JOSÉ M. DE MESA
New Rituals Through AIDS   21
  JAN RUIJTER

II · Traditional Responses and Questions to the
     Tradition   31
The Reaction of the Citizens of La Seu d'Urgell to the Black
  Death   33
  ALBERT VILLARÓ
Lamentation and Mass Death   42
  ANDRÉS TORRES QUEIRUGA
God at the Heart of Hell: From Theodicy to the Word
  of the Cross   53
  MICHEL DENEKEN
The Language of Remembrance: Reflections on
  Theological Discussion of the Phenomenon of Mass Death   65
  WERNER JEANROND

III · Keeping Memory   75
When Remembering Brings Redemption: Faith and the
  Armenian Genocide   77
  VIGEN GUROIAN

Dead but Still Missing: Mothers of Plaza de Mayo
    Transform Argentina   89
    MARY E. HUNT
The Dissonant Sounds of Hope: The Music of Mass
    Death and Christian Liturgical Remembrance   97
    RICHARD N. FRAGOMENI
Commemorations   106
    DAVID N. POWER

IV · Conclusions for Liturgical Remembrance   109
Calling Up the Dead   111
    DAVID N. POWER

Special Column   121

Contributors   124

Editorial

The Spectre of Mass Death

At the time that it was decided to compose an issue of *Concilium* dealing with how liturgy responds to mass death, we were in the wake of the Gulf War. In newspapers, in magazines and on television screens people the world over had seen pictures of the 'corridor of death'. Iraqi soldiers in their hordes lay dead in the silence of the desert, sometimes trapped in the charred remains of their motorized vehicles, sometimes cut down on foot as they tried to escape from air strikes. No matter how much people wanted to see the troops of Saddam Hussein expelled from Kuwait, there seemed something wanton and frightening beyond naming in this mass death. Now as we are editing the articles, what the world is watching are the process of 'ethnic cleansing' in Bosnia and the pictures of emaciated bodies lying in the fields, in the houses and in the streets of Somalia. There is a high likelihood that when the review appears, some other gruesome spectacle will have captured our attention.

Several times in the course of a year, the news media report deaths in their hundreds or thousands as a result of earthquake, tidal waves, transport disasters, cruel fighting or famine. Through mass communication, people in our age are amply if superficially informed of these tragedies. In the Western world especially, the bombardment of information is such that the events are trivialized or consciousness numbed. On the other hand, despite the danger of making tragedy banal, there is a public sensitivity to the numbers who die as a result of political oppression, more awareness of the numbers who have died or continue to die in this century as a result of war, and an uneasiness about death from such realities as AIDS or drugs. In one way or another, the public is brought face to face with mass death. People witness a series or quantity of deaths which defy counting, threaten the victims with anonymity, and leave survivors benumbed as much as grieving. The collective consciousness is troubled by what seems absurd, without reason, in these deaths. It either blocks out the reality or searches hard for ways in which to give it meaning. Among those who react, vigils or symbolic actions or demonstrations of concern of one sort or another are organized, but the worship in our churches is often no further disturbed than by a bland inclusion in the prayer of the faithful, names of persons and places possibly mispronounced.

In his well-known study of the history of death, *The Hour of Our Death*, Philippe Ariès has dubbed eras with such names as the age of tame death, of the death of the self, or of invisible death, thus trying to express the prevailing cultural attitudes to the experience of death. In our day, one might well speak of an age of absurd death. The many deaths in World War I that seemed quite senseless, the Holocaust of the Jewish people under the Nazi régime, the deaths of soldiers and citizens in Vietnam and Cambodia, death by famine in a world filled with plenty, the tortuous death of victims of political and military institutions, the slow and painful dying of AIDS patients, all touch death with a note of absurdity. Not only is it without reason, but too often it is brought on by the meaningless, vicious or more prosaically callous behaviour of human societies. And it always opens up in the heart the question of the absence of God.

The burial of the victims of mass death has its own language. In the cases of human atrocity, such as of death in extermination camps, or of the hidden death of a régime's victims where the people simply 'disappear', or of death in war, there is no ritual at all to mark the hour of death. The dead are left nameless. In other cases, as in death by famine or natural catastrophe, it is a matter of hurriedly burying the dead, lest disease set in. Ritual is perfunctory and the individual body becomes one of many, left to lie nameless as it were in a mass grave.

The personal and collective need to mark these deaths more meaningfully remains. There is the search for some public act to give name and sense to the persons and their dying. In the aftermath of tragedy, families and other survivors look for ways of remembering. Paradoxically, those who die almost anonymously have to be given a public image if the culture is to overcome its wound. There is a variety to the rituals to which people have resort, for they may be cultural, political, or religious, or a mix of all three elements.

In church ritual, as elsewhere, the absurd has to be named as the necessary route to the retrieval of life and meaning, even for the dead. Church congregations and church ministers know that the commemoration of the dead under such circumstances cannot be met with the customary liturgies, nor the anguish of survivors met with traditional religious answers. Finding apt celebration and apt modes of commemoration requires inventiveness. It is not only from within the liturgical repertory that the imagination is moved, but believers may find much that is rich and healing in other forms of commemoration.

While the ultimate concern of this issue of *Concilium* is the quest for Christian liturgies that have resonance in this age of absurd death, in face of mass death, it was planned in the realization that such worship is given birth within a culture, as part of a larger social endeavour to commemorate and ritualize. It was also planned in the painful awareness that standard Christian responses to mass death, or even to death itself, are called into question. Theological issues arise that have to be faced even in the process of coming to more adequate ritual and liturgical forms of mourning and commemorating the dead.

Hence in the first part of the issue, writers look to current experiences of burying the dead in the midst of catastrophe. Death by famine in Africa (Semporé), the destruction consequent on natural calamities in the Philippines (di Mesa), and the daily roster of those who die from AIDS (Ruijter), are three very different realities. They are, however, among the various calamities of our age which face us with this gruesome reality. The writers point out that prayer is impossible unless some attention is given to the reasons and causes for disaster. Ethical issues, even of a global nature, inevitably surface when faced with the tragic need to bury the victims of mass death.

In the second part, writers look at standard Christian ways of naming death and expressing the hope of survival in the light of this reality. These articles provide a historical example (Villaró), a look at the use of lamentation (Torres Queiruga), a discussion of theological suppositions (Deneken), and a consideration of the employment of imaginative patterns of Christian language (Jeanrond).

In the third part, attention is given to episodes that already belong in the past. Authors (Guroian, Fragomeni, Hunt) give accounts of various ways whereby in looking back to instances of mass death communities or peoples in different cultures have devised forms of keeping memory.

These articles show how a people must deal with the memory which includes death's absurdity and the cruelty and anonymity which mark death's circumstances. They also show how imaginative creativity can call up the dead so that they have a new place in social and cultural life and how this kind of remembrance becomes a social force confronting unjust or oppressive actions and ideologies. This would also be the place to gather information about ways of keeping memory of the victims of mass or absurd death in different countries or sub-groups around the world, as is indicated in the brief note by David Power. Though the articles in this section of the issue, and the rituals and symbols here mentioned, are not about liturgies, they offer instructive patterns for liturgical commemoration, and reflect how liturgical commemoration would be misplaced if not accompanied by the creative imagination and action which bear on social realities.

A final editorial article by David Power attempts to offer a more comprehensive picture of what is at stake for Christian communities when faced with mass death and offers some reflections on keeping liturgical commemoration of the event and of the victims. It has not been the purpose to offer an ideal liturgy, one that can go into the liturgical books, as it were. The hope is more simply that from the materials offered in the volume, diverse communities may find hope and find their imaginations sparked to a hope-filled commemoration of the living dead in an age of absurd death.

David N. Power
F. Kabasele Lumbala

even the most humble to be able to cleanse themselves by themselves alone. Salvation must come from the outside – there appears to be no other way.

The Bible is so full of human stories, but the Christian tradition of the West has, for all practical purposes, replaced them with philosophical theories and formulae, as if God's way of revealing through human stories and sensual imagery was not really critical and serious enough and we had to improve on it. Isn't this typical of our Western mentality: always trying to improve on what the other is doing, even if the other is God! This is so typical of our Western arrogance which always seeks to impose our way upon all others as the only way which is authentic and true. We have given our lives for the sake of others, but we have not been able to accept as legitimate and true the otherness of the others! This is still one of our strongest characteristics of the West: our inability to value difference – especially religious difference – in a positive, respectful and accepting way. This was the great sin which marked the beginning of the new world order in 1492 and it continues to be the great sin of the West today: we the Western Christians *versus* all the other pagan and heathen peoples of the world. This is precisely the great contribution that is coming out of the marginalized, crucified and silenced peoples of the Third World: a call for a deep metanoia from the 'we versus you' to a new 'we' that can truly welcome and include everyone in their otherness.

It is from this perspective that we dare to produce one more contribution on Christ in Asia, drawing from some of the various theological groupings of that continent. It is the effort of the Third World section of *Concilium* to continue to open doors for a more fruitful dialogue that will further the process of a truly world fellowship of believers. Is there room for Christ in Asia? We ask the question from within the Asian perspective, but in reality it is a universal question for all Christian churches. Is there room for Christ in the present world order? The answer would appear to be a quick and unequivocal yes. But is the answer too easy? Let us probe deeper into the provocative problematic that is posed to all Christians by our Asian sisters and brothers. One of the greatest accomplishments of the 500th year of the new world order is that the voice of the broken, enslaved and silenced victims is beginning to be heard around the world. From the crucified peoples of the world, the new word of grace and salvation is being proclaimed. It is the gospel that is being written by the hands crushed and calloused by hard labour, and proclaimed by the tongues parched and dried up by the lack of water or food that is today unmasking the unsuspected idols of Western Christianity. This is liberating colonizing Christianity from its cultural arrogance and enslavements, purifying it of its decaying elements and ennobling it by allowing the most authentic traits of the true Christian tradition of the Gospels to shine through. A new Christianity is being born out of the broken bodies and spilled blood of the victims of the present world order. Is there room for this Christ in our Christian churches and theologates of the present world order?

As Christians of the former colonized peoples begin to struggle with their independence, the question of religious identity becomes of the utmost importance. Is the religion of the colonial missioners the ultimate acceptance of colonial domination, or can it now become, once purified of its colonial aspects, the hidden energy of new movements of recognition, respect, acceptance and new life? As Pieris brings out, the Christ who is emerging in Asia today is not the 'accomplice Christ' who in any way justifies invasion, domination or injustice of any type, but the 'victim-judge' who in solidarity with the victims of the sinful systems – civil, cultural or religious – of today's Asia demands a conversion of Asian societies to Christ's order along the *via crucis* of greedless sharing. This is certainly happening among the Dalits of India, the Minjung Feminine Christa of Korea (unfortunately this article by Hyung Kyung of Seoul never arrived), the Communists of China who in 1920 perceived in the stories of Jesus of Nazareth a new power for spiritual regeneration of China, the landless peoples of the Philippines struggling for new life.

'. . . laid him in a manger, because there was no room for them . . . ' (Luke 2.7). Anyone would be honoured to welcome a famous, well-known and notable personality into their midst. But who wants to welcome an untouchable? A smelly, disfigured, unknown from one of the ugly regions of society! The shepherds who were among the social outcasts, the broken untouchables of their society, recognized his glory immediately. But the structures of Jerusalem became very disturbed by his arrival and ended up by driving him out of the city to Calvary. There is no room for Jesus of Nazareth, the Christ, in the sinful systems of any culture or society. This very Jesus who from his brokenness and nothingness invites us all into fellowship with him and one another is the true Christ of the Scriptures. This is the very Jesus that the untouchables of India recognized as their liberating Saviour in 1910. The ultimate Christness of Jesus of Nazareth in life was his non-Christness of the post-resurrection reflections. His total kenosis and identification with the scum, untouchable and rejected of society in their existential shame, scandal and brokenness even to execution as a criminal deprived him of all earthly dignity, honour and glory. It is this obedient non-Christness that gives way to the post-Easter christological titles of glory and praise and eventually to the Western confusion of seeing him as imaged in the triumphant emperor.

Christianity was born in Asia, but as it progressed into the Hellenized

I · Burying the Dead in the Midst of Disaster

The Famine in Africa

Sidbe Semporé

'They grope in search of the entrance to a cemetery' (Albert Londre)

Let's have the honesty to say it: in the face of the ravages of famine in eastern and southern Africa today, it might seem somewhat indecent to evoke in a few pages the hideous face of the spectre which is devouring the living flesh of the African continent by the million, above all when the author of this article and his readers are sheltered from the torments of hunger. The only justification is for the evocation of this scandal of our time to revolt us in heart and mind and drive us body and soul to a radical and immediate repentance in our behaviour.

The tragic truth about the ravages of hunger in Africa and elsewhere in the world is that all human beings, wherever they may be, are involved in it by virtue of our common humanity. That common humanity creates in all of us bonds, rights and duties of solidarity towards those who are fainting away with hunger at the gates or the frontiers.

The facts

Birds hide in order to die. The intolerable and revolting spectacle of reporters and cameramen who, with no regard for that part of humanity brooding under dead flesh and dried-out bones, throw as food to the voracious media the dying groans of skeletons on the point of extinction and the farewell to the world of children with bloated bellies, helps to anaesthetize the consciences of television viewers which are already saturated and repulsed. Can the evocation of the tragic situation of famine-stricken Africa given here have any better effect?

In October 1991, the weekly report of the International Monetary Fund on 'World Economic Perspectives' stated that, for Africa, 'around thirty million inhabitants of this region are at risk from famine, above all in

Ethiopia and the Sudan, but also in Angola, Burkina Faso, Liberia, Mozambique and Somalia.' Two months later, and down to the present day, the international media have been relaying the cry of anguish from the countries of southern Africa and Madagascar which have been struck by a catastrophic drought, directly threatening twenty million inhabitants with death from famine. In June-July 1992, some countries in the Sahel in turn complained of a severe lack of rain and cried for help.

The report of experts for the year 1992 is terrible: between twenty-five and thirty million people, for the most part children, are directly in mortal danger as a result of the famine which is raging over the African continent, and sixty million are likely to be the victims of severe malnutrition. This apocalyptic situation, which results from complex human and climatic factors, is a particularly dramatic repetition of cataclysms similar to those in the distant and more recent past of Africa. There is no need to refer here to the biblical accounts of famine in Egypt to see how the scourge of famine has always intermittently threatened the fragile societies of Africa.

Through stories of migrations and oral traditions, most of the peoples of the continent preserve the memory, years afterwards, of the 'lean cows', the time when they were reduced to gnawing at roots and fainting with hunger in front of dried-up wells. However, the last two decades (1970–1990) must count among the most murderous in the history of contemporary Africa. One might recall the terrible drought which struck the whole band of the Sahel from the Cap Verde islands to Ethiopia at the end of the 1970s and decimated the populations by hundreds of thousands. Since then, the Sahel has undergone an accelerated degradation of its soil and climate, and the galloping desertification is causing major population movements and a constant influx of refugees who are driven to neighbouring countries for economic reasons. The fragile economies of these poor countries, mortally stricken by endemic climatic cataclysms, have to cope with constant shortages. In spite of the courage of the country people, many forms of international aid, cries of distress and calls for help on behalf of millions of victims of disaster and starvation from the states of the Sahel increase year by year. Year by year the scourge of famine increases its ravages despite the improvement in some economic or climatic factors, and international aid, whether for a particular crisis or in a more permanent form.

The tragedy of Somalia

Can one example stand for all? The situations are so different from one region to another in Africa, and the map of famine changes to such a degree from year to year, that one should avoid hasty generalizations beginning from specific cases. The past decade has seen the suffering of countries like the Sahel, Ethiopia and the Sudan. The 1990s began with serious shortages of grain and the ravages caused to the harvest by the exceptional drought in southern Africa and the Horn of Africa, and by the civil war in Liberia, Djibouti, Mozambique and Somalia.

What is happening in this last country defies understanding and points an accusing finger at human consciences. 'This country, totally ravaged by war and by famine, looks as if an atomic bomb has been dropped on it', exclaimed a horrified visitor. As I write, few people are making statements or taking a stand on the situation in Somalia, and it is given little attention on the media, since the attention and aid of the Western world is so concentrated on the conflict in Yugoslavia. Three reactions from officials should be enough to indicate the totality of the disaster in which Somalia has been submerged since 1991. First of all Mohamed Sahnoun, United Nations special envoy in Somalia. On 3 August 1992 he declared:

> Because there has been no international involvement and a lack of funds, it is perhaps already too late to save the 1.5 million people in Somalia – almost a quarter of the population – doomed to die in the immediate future unless there is massive food aid.

After a short visit to Somalia, Bernard Louchner, French minister of health and welfare, wrote on 6 August 1992:

> I have seen nothing worse since Biafra. I have discovered death. The death of a country and above all the death of these children who are perishing on the roads.

He appealed to Europe and the international community to make sure that the conflict in Yugoslavia did not obscure the terrible drama in Somalia.

That same day an interview appeared in the German newspaper *Die Zeit* with the Secretary-General of the United Nations, Boutros Boutros-Ghali. In it he forcibly reiterated his indignation at the lack of commitment from the rich countries to saving Somalia:

> There is a difference between the civil wars in Somalia and in Yugoslavia. In Somalia ten times as many people are being killed as in Yugoslavia, but no one is interested in this country. Compared with Somalia, the conflict in Yugoslavia is a war of the rich. The United

Nations and the Secretary-General must devote the same attention to each of the member states.

Echoing these three declarations, the aim of which was to shake the apathy over the death of a whole people, on 9 August 1992 Bill Clinton, then Democrat candidate in the presidential elections, asked for the American administration to be more involved in the humanitarian action of the United Nations on behalf of Somalia. In fact out of a total population of 7.5 million, 4.5 million are estimated as being at long-term danger from famine.

In the camps, on average one Somali dies every minute, most of them children. Up to mid-August 1992 only a tenth of the aid necessary for the survival of the populations had reached the country, while the United Nations had yet to send the 500 'soldiers of peace' meanly assigned to the protection of food aid.

Is famine a matter of fate?

Why then this chronic and permanent degradation of the food situation in so many African countries?

Climatic reasons

First of all, one feels, we must blame heaven – in despair! Heaven, i.e. God and the divine powers which refuse fertile dew to the land. It is quite common to see governments calling for the prayers and vows of the churches and believers in the most serious climatic catastrophes.

But it should not be forgotten that heaven is more prosaically the firmament of clouds which drop rain and over which human beings as yet have no control. Thus in Somalia the rainfall has been insufficient since 1989, and the harvests almost non-existent. Worse, even when the heavens prove clement, the harvests are sometimes totally destroyed by clouds of locusts. Finally, the inexorable advance of the desert into the Sahel, despite campaigns of reforestation and increased construction of dams, is reducing cultivable areas and accelerating the degradation of the soil.

Human causes

I do not know whether one can follow the French agronomist René Dumont and some eco-systematicians in pointing to the Western countries and America in particular as being chiefly responsible for the atmospheric disturbances and the unbalancing of the climate of the planet: 'The industrialized countries and America are the chief culprits for the destruction of the ozone layer, and consequently for the drought in Africa, Madagascar and elsewhere in the world,' he stated after the Rio summit.[1]

One thing is certain: human beings are largely responsible for the famine in Africa.

The impact of modern civilization and the Western powers on the course of African history has profoundly affected the structures of subsistence and caused an upheaval in the modes of production. The creation of wholly artificial states, forcing mosaics of people to live together under the banner of the myth of the nation and the ideology of the party, is a tragic historical error, as is shown by the millions of deaths in Biafra, Katanga, Ethiopia, the Sudan, the Western Sahara, Cabinda, Casamance, Ruanda, Burundi and Somalia. To foist these structures from another world on fragile African societies leads to counterfeits and caricatures of states in which 'the frontier' makes the citizen a prisoner and the foreigner an enemy. Foodstuff, subject to strict customs regulations, no longer circulates from one country to another, from one region to another – for reasons of state!

On the other hand, since the colonial era cultures based on exploitation and the demand for a return on investment – often monocultures – have exploited Africa for the benefit of the industrialized countries and to the detriment of food-producing cultures. Now the world market of agricultural products has not only strangled the African economy by the unjust and fradulent pricing of raw matrials, but has again severely penalized the African farmer by the payment of massive subsidies to farmers and exporters in Western countries.[2]

Finally, the weight of external debt (200 billion dollars for the whole of Africa south of the Sahara), the servicing of the debt and the programmes of structural adjustment imposed on these economies sucked dry by the banks and world financial institutions, hardly encourage getting an effective grasp on food needs. However, it would be unfair to put responsibility for the misfortunes of the African agricultural sector only on the international situation. As early as the 1960s René Dumont, in his famous work *L'Afrique noire est mal partie*, was warning African leaders against unrealistic political choices which neglected the vital sector of agriculture.

Today, in almost all the African countries, the populations are paying dearly for these political errors and rash economic options which have changed countries like Nigeria, Guinea, Mali and the Ivory Coast from being exporters of grain into indebted importers.

The majority of governments chose the wrong priority, preferring to sacrifice agriculture and the countryfolk at the expense of prestige projects – the scandalous white elephants of the African cities – and a minority of privileged people. Worse, the administrative system and the educational model made a major contribution to depreciating and devaluing agricultural work and depopulating the villages, in favour of the shanty towns of the great cities.

As a result, the African agricultural sector is nowadays characterized by archaic technology and methods, by the non-existence of internal or regional systems for stocking, exchanging and marketing products, by the absence of an agricultural policy and the rational exploitation of land.

The degradation of the environment by deforestation, the uncontrolled cutting down of wood for fires, and in some regions brushwood fires, lead to a loss of fertile land and seasonal rain.

On the other hand, the present situation in Ethiopia, Somalia, Sudan, Liberia and Mozambique is evidence that the incessant conflicts which bathe the continent in blood are one of the major causes of the scourge of famine. Is it conceivable that in a decade millions of individuals should have been confronted with famine in a gigantic 'granary of Africa' like the Sudan? The flow of millions of half-starved refugees, parked in makeshift camps, perishing on the way or setting themselves adrift on deadly rafts, is a terrible scandal for the Africa of nations and tribes. A million dead in Mozambique since civil war was unleashed in 1975 and, in 1992, 800,000 people threatened with famine and two million refugees depending on international aid to survive: that is a record which strips all legitimacy from those who hold power in this country and their adversaries who kill in order to get rid of them. It is the same in Somalia, where refugees are digging communal graves in the camps to bury the hundreds of people who are dying of hunger every day. The absurdity of the phenomenon of refugees in Africa still appears in this vicious double circle: in October 1991 Ethiopia was sheltering 385,000 refugees from Sudan while Sudan was receiving 663,000 from Ethiopia. At the same time there were 355,000 Somali refugees in Ethiopia and 350,000 Ethiopians in Somalia. The height of cruelty is reached by the governments and the rebel movements in Ethiopia, Somalia, the Sudan and Mozambique, who do not hesitate to make use of hunger as a weapon in the fratricidal wars in which they are engaged, burning harvests, turning away international aid, or preventing any intervention on the part of humanitarian organizations. Not to mention the colossal sum invested by one or the other in the purchase of arms or munitions.

Finally, among the human factors leading to famine in Africa, mention must be made of the uncontrolled demographic growth which, in the present political and economic context, heightens the existing imbalance between production and consumption, and aggravates the situation of malnutrition on the continent. The effort made by governments to educate people and motivate a change of behaviour still appear too timid. In countries where young people under the age of twenty-one form a majority of 65% of the population, the social situation becomes explosive when unemployment, far from prompting the young to return to the land, makes them the prey of social scourges. The gap – an ever increasing gap – between demographic growth and economic growth is soon likely to make the food crisis even worse.

This list of the main causes of famine in Africa leads to the conclusion that famine is never an unavoidable fate. The main factors in famine derive above all from human behaviour. It is perhaps easier to ward off endemic famine brought about by climatic calamities than to conquer the structural famine caused by human behaviour and action. Must we give way to pessimism? Human and religious ethics are a great help in this struggle against famine and despair.

'Take and eat all of you . . .'

What if the Good News for the millions of starving people in Africa is summed up in this succinct testament of Jesus: 'Take and eat all of you . . .'? In fact, everything throughout the teaching of Jesus ('I was hungry . . .', Matt. 25) and in his work of doing good ('I have pity on this crowd because they have nothing to eat,' Mark 8.2) shows that he took very seriously, not 'the problem of famine in Israel', but the need for human beings to eat their fill. The Good News to the poor is proclaimed in the form of bread multiplied (Mark 8), begged for (Matt. 11), given (John 6), broken (Matt. 26.26); in the image of the banquet in which people eat to the full, together (Luke 14.15). A re-reading of the gospel in the middle of a refugee camp, before half-starved people who are going to lose their lives for want of 'bread', by the fault of both heaven and earth, gives flesh and breath to the words of the one who, to save humanity from want, made himself 'bread' for the life of the world. The passion of the starving in Africa and elsewhere sends us, beyond humanitarian principals and moral precepts, to the violent and searing reality of the paschal meal, and to the brutal efficacy of the sin of the world.

Confronted with the drama of famine in Africa, in the name of human justice and the principles of the gospel, one can fight against the selfishness of the well-to-do. The structural sin often denounced in the cold mechanisms of the world economy and international geopolitics operates openly with no pity for the weak. The injustice which characterizes relations between Africa, exploited, pillaged and cheated by powerful nations, and the rich countries which give it the crumbs from their table is flagrant. A new world order is being constructed against the little ones and the poor. The regional regroupings made in Europe and North America and the national redeployments taking place within the old Soviet galaxy are sounding the knell of Third World ideas of co-operation between North and South.

The desertion of Africa, more and more 'forgotten' by its old colonizers, has now begun. People are indignant, but what is the use? The European community imposes quotas of food production on member countries to reduce the enormously excessive stocks of food and to stabilize prices. Here and there the farmers protest by destroying the crops. It has been calculated that 100 million undernourished human beings could be fed with 2% of the world production of wheat. The High Commission for Refugees has for a long time been calling for $55 million for the repatriation of Angolan refugees; it has obtained only $2 million, and the Angolans must stay in exile. One dare not quantify the colossal investment made in the Olympic Games held in Barcelona in July and August 1992 by nations which can offer 'bread and circuses' in abundance, just to spare the '3 billion television viewers' the unbearable image of the long calvary of starving people. But groaning or repenting for others is no use. Africa does not identify itself only with Lazarus lying beneath the world's table. It is trampled on by its own children. Its sin is that of the world: the starving and the malnourished bear witness to it. When one knows that hunger not only threatens the survival of millions of beings but goes on to leave an indelible mark on the faculties of possible survivors and permanently weakens whole generations, one can see the enormous responsibility of those who provoke it, encourage it, support it or turn their backs on it.

Primum vivere, 'life comes first', said the Romans. The governments and the churches cannot opt out of the first precept of human existence. And if this precept, which gives every human being the right to food and the essentials of existence, has in the past taken the inadequate form of 'alms' and 'charity' in religion, it nevertheless remains engraved indelibly on the human side.

The eucharist signifies and reactualizes this cardinal precept of the right to life and the right to food, the right to the bread of the earth which allows one to welcome the bread of heaven. 'Man does not live by bread alone but by every word which proceeds from the mouth of God.' The word of God cannot feed beings stripped of their humanity, reduced to anonymous objects of charity, with a hypothetical survival of primary functions as their one horizon. 'A starving belly has no ears', not even for the word of God.

It is high time that we took account, in Africa, of the indecency of a certain conception of the eucharist and a certain way of celebrating it which is an insult to the inalienable right of the starving. 'One does not talk about rope in the home of a hanged man.' How can we go on giving to communities of starving and undernourished people this talk about fasting and refreshment, distributing grammes of unleavened bread and suggesting 'reservation' to poor beings who do not have one meal a day? In Africa, the ritual quarrels and controversies over the eucharistic substance must result in the commitment of the churches in the struggle against hunger and its causes still proving marginal.

The Catholic Church in Africa has a great temptation to reduce the eucharist to this 'true bread of angels which descends from heaven for us and which we all adore'. Now the starving of Africa, 'parcels of eucharist reliving permanently the passion of Christ',[3] call for the understanding of the church in its practice of the sacrament of the bread of life.

In contact with them, the Lord's Supper truly becomes an anamnesis of the drama of life which sends the church and believers back:

To the earth which nourishes them, where Christians mysteriously join countryfolk in their earthly passion, in their daily anguish and their quest for 'bread'. Can the church validly 'break bread', in other words share, in the name of the Risen Christ, the fruit of the labour and toil of African peasants without actively taking their side for the improvement of living and working conditions? Feeding the hungry is also something which arises from the sacramental words of the Lord's Supper, 'Take and eat'. The bread shared with the saviour sends us back, by a demand of incarnation, to the bread of the poor of the earth, those who produce it and those who lack it.

To the warehouses of the merchants and traders, where the grain is stocked, manipulated and trafficked. Eucharistic 'sharing' 'points the church to the bottlenecks where bread ceases to be for all'. Then, in the name of the unbounded liberality of the saving bread, the church is called on to engage in the struggle against those who starve the people and do not hesitate to produce famine artificially to boost their own interests. As long as 'self-sufficiency in food' and the 'free circulation of goods' remain empty slogans, numerous Africans will continue to die of hunger beside full granaries.

To the international economic circuits, symbols both of humanity working without a frontier through humanitarian organizations and organisms for the survival of the disinheritance and the inhumanity of the rich who impose their law and their prices. Those to whom it is said in Ps. 14.4, 'When they eat their bread, it is my people that they eat!' The breaking of the eucharistic bread opens up the horizon of a universal brotherhood in which 'bread' has no frontiers because it is withdrawn from the appetite of speculators and trusts. For the starving of Africa, love has the countenance of shared bread. Does the eucharist incarnate a more fundamental message?

Translated by John Bowden

Notes

1. So far no study has been published on the possible effect of the third French nuclear test in the Sahara (January 1961) on the environment and climate south of the Sahara.

2. In the 12–18 March 1992 issue of the Paris weekly *Jeune Afrique*, 1627, 68–9, Sophie Bessis noted that 'thanks to the aid given to producers, European grain or American rice proved to be cheaper in Dakar or Bamko than local grain. That aggravates the dependence of African countries for the foodstuffs that they consume without being able to produce them in sufficient quantities, while millet and sorgum are more and more disdained there . . . The programmed lack of discipline in the prices of base products and the disloyal competition which delivers Africa into the hands of the major world exporters of food contribute towards aggravating the crisis of which it is a victim.'

3. A saying of Fr Joseph Wresinsky about the Fourth World.

Burying the Victims of Natural Disasters in the Philippines

José M. de Mesa

Earthquakes and typhoons are part of life in the Philippines. The former seldom occur, the latter traverse the islands annually. But the earthquake which struck the northern region of Luzon island on 16 July 1990 and the typhoon of 5 November 1991 which hit a city and its environs in the south of the country are remembered with sorrow for bringing death to so many and destroying so much. Focusing on these two will provide adequate starting points for a discussion of the Filipino experience of natural disaster. Because both have occurred among lowland Filipinos who share a common culture, we are in a good position to look closely at an aspect of Christian life within a homogeneous cultural group.

The July 1990 earthquake had an intensity of 7.7 on the Richter scale. Dubbed the 'killer quake', this tremor led to the death of at least 500 people, most of them crushed, hit or pinned down by structures which had collapsed. The latter event, the typhoon of November 1991, brought continuous rains and caused flash floods mainly in the city of Ormoc as deep as twelve feet in many places and around twenty feet in low-lying areas. When the water finally receded, about 5,000 bloated corpses were found scattered throughout the city. Most of the dead were the poor who were living near the river banks, places considered high-risk areas in Ormoc.

I. The experience

A. *Relief and rehabilitation*

In both disasters it was the search and care for survivors that were attended to first. Relief distribution was immediately organized. Individuals and groups, including parishes, throughout the country helped in any way they could. To prevent the outbreak of an epidemic, the dead had to be found and buried. The scattered corpses in different stages of decomposition in Ormoc City were literally collected in trucks and dumped into common graves as soon as possible. There was neither time to identify all the bodies nor to bury them with appropriate rites.

Attention was also given to the psychological and social aspects of the calamities. A Catholic high school, for instance, organized sessions for its students and their parents to process their traumatic experiences related to the earthquake. The co-operative effort by some people to help survivors cope psychologically in another place led to the formation of a self-help co-operative which extended relief services. Psychologists and counsellors had much to do in Ormoc. A priest reminiscing about the disaster there said, 'People roamed around without direction, helpless and dislocated'. He recalled how some victims rushed to pack their things at the slightest shower, while others tended to withdraw, remain quiet or stay idle.

B. Christian prayer and liturgy

In contrast to the organized relief and rehabilitation services rendered by the church, very little was done to respond in a contextual manner to the specifically religious dimension of the tragedies through prayer and critical reflection. The usual blessing and mass for the dead were undertaken. Where a personal touch was wanting, it was supplied by the personal devotion and prayer of those who grieved. However, no special liturgies were formulated to lay to rest the victims of the two disasters. The eucharist, as soon as it was feasible to celebrate it, was carried out in the usual manner of the Roman rite. Basically the same words, the same gestures, the same ritual were utilized. The only accommodation the celebration showed to what had happened were the relevant introductions, prayers of the faithful as well as the homilies. Apparently, what was true in the areas affected by the calamities was also true, as a rule, throughout the country in other Catholic communities which remembered the victims in prayer.

It is understandable that the pressure of multitudinous tasks arising from crises pre-empted creativity, which could have made liturgy contextually meaningful. But one can ask why nothing was done about original liturgies afterwards, when the situations were gradually returning to normal. Not much productive thought was employed, probably because the mass was the mass. The eternal liturgy goes on regardless of what happens. Besides, the celebration depended upon priests, even in instances when people might have wanted more meaningful and contextual celebrations and could have done something about them.

Situationally relevant worship and prayer materialized outside officially designated forms. Most likely because these happened outside of the officially prescribed rites, the celebrations were easily joint efforts of Catholics and Protestants. Called 'ecumenical services', these forms of worship remembered the dead in prayer and reminded the living of their responsibilities. They gave expression to sorrow as well as to renewed hope. A couple of examples are in order.

These were the first anniversary commemoration of the 16 July earthquake held in a town plaza in the North and a 'Day of Mourning' service in Ormoc City on the fortieth day after the disaster struck. The former remembered the dead through prayer, the tolling of church bells and the re-enactment of peoples' experience of the earthquake. Word, symbol and gesture reminded people of those whose lives were cut short by a disaster. The service was not only meant to remember the dead; it was also intended to remind the living of the need for concerted action to rebuild life. Hence the theme of the celebration was 'Reshaping Our Shattered Communities Towards Solidarity in Action'.

The theme of mourning was much more pronounced in community prayer in Ormoc. Sufficiently freed from the urgent demands of relief for survivors and immediate burial of the decomposing corpses, people gathered together for a whole day of mourning. It was the fortieth day since the catastrophe happened. The day was marked with much prayer from the break of dawn until early evening. There was a procession, at which most of the worst affected areas became stations where people would stop and pray for those who died. These places were then blessed by priests.

After this procession, an ecumenical service which lasted for five hours was held. This service revolved around the importance of ecology and the responsibility of Christians to care for the earth, although it included the commemoration of the dead in prayer and in the laying of wreaths. Once again, the themes of mourning and renewal of commitment to life were put together. The dead and the living were commemorated. The day of mourning ended with the celebration of the eucharist by the Catholic community in the cemetery, where all the bodies which had been found scattered throughout the city were buried together in haste.

C. Traditional practices

Mourning and remembrance for those who perished in these disasters did not end soon after their deaths, if we consider the traditions in the

Philippines related to burying the dead. It is customary for bereaved families to have a novena for the dead after the burial. The final day of the novena is capped by a small celebration. Similarly, the fortieth day of death is an occasion for the extended family and friends to gather together for prayer and some celebration. The year immediately after the death is a year of mourning. Members of the immediate family of the dead ordinarily wear a sign of mourning, usually a black pin. At the end of that year, relatives and friends are usually invited to come together for prayer in memory of the dead person and, again, for some celebration. Death anniversaries are observed in a number of ways: a visit to the grave, a mass for the dead in church, or family prayer before the altar at home. The dead are remembered time and again, especially during the yearly traditional visits of families to the tombs of their beloved dead on the Feast of All Saints, 1 November. On this day cemeteries in the Philippines are crowded with people, and the occasion displays a festive as well as a prayerful mood. Such visits to the cemeteries normally become opportunities for family reunions. Here, as in the other practices related to the commemoration of the dead, we find the same intertwining of the realities of the dead and the living which we have seen earlier.

D. Religious reading of the disasters

Experience is necesarily interpreted experience. Analysis of the religious perception of the tragedies reveals what had been experienced by people in general. In their minds God caused the disasters. This is not just a defective Christian understanding, but rather the way Filipinos believe, as they have believed even before the advent of Christianity. God's existence and the identification of what happens in the world with God's will are cultural presuppositions. God's sovereignty and might and its counterpart, human submission and vulnerability, are largely unquestioned.[1] God who loans life to us can take it back at any time. The comment of one earthquake survivor is illustrative: 'I was so shocked because upon running out, we saw the building collapse and (there was a) report (of) instances of death inside. We saw a lot of people crying outside, shouting for help. It was an experience . . . I am alive, our house is still intact, my family is alive, while others died. Is this divine providence? Yes, I think so!'

It was widely believed that the disaster was God's way of punishing people for their wickedness. In Baguio City people talked about hotels where gambling and marital infidelity found havens crashing down. Where Catholic churches and schools sustained the most damage from the earthquake, people spoke of God's wrath as both chastisement and reminder. People had to pay for their sinfulness. Hence, people prayed during the earthquake, some even publicly on the streets. They asked for mercy and petitioned for another chance to live better. The catastrophe was also regarded as the divine way of reminding people to return to the path of salvation. One Catholic priest in his homily said, 'The lesson for each and every one of us who survived is: we were given another chance! What will we do with it?' The survivors were to consider themselves blessed for getting another chance.

While there was an unquestioning acceptance of God's judgment and sanction in general, there were also individuals who faulted God for what had actually come to pass. Some persons in the Ormoc disaster cursed God for making them still live. Others blamed God for having allowed this to happen. But whether the attitude was one of resignation to, or of complaint against, the divine will, God was perceived to be responsible for the calamities. Tridentine Catholic teaching, which is still widely held in the Philippines, only reinforced and legitimated this deeply ingrained cultural understanding of God, instead of challenging it. It spoke of submission in all things to the divine will and pleasure, and exhorted Catholics to 'remember that if by prayers and supplication we are not delivered from evil, we should endure our afflictions with patience, convinced that it is the will of God that we should endure them'.[2]

There were Christians, on the other hand, who experienced the earthquake and the typhoon differently from a religious perspective. They believed that these natural disasters were not willed by God. God was not being punitive: people had become irresponsible by severely damaging their natural environment. These voices stressed the issue of ecology and human responsibility for the earth (cf. *Gaudium et Spes*, 55). One Christian-inspired group explicitly stated that 'to many of us, the killer quake was Nature's way of taking revenge for our wanton destruction, abuse, misuse and neglect of Mother Earth'. Responding to the religious question raised by the earthquake, another pastor assured people in a sermon that God does not like 'to play a joke on us by shaking us out of our senses'. But 'if we tinker with the ecosystem or the balance of nature and trample upon the integrity of creation' he warned, 'we cannot escape nature's fury and vengeance.' A focussed lesson-plan in religion on all levels of a Catholic girls' school also dealt with the specifically religious aspects of the earthquake disaster. The gist of it was a scientific explanation of earthquakes, the issue of ecology and human responsibility for the environment. It emphasized the point that the disaster which they had witnessed was not God's will. Even a pastor who was pleased with the increased attendance and collection in his church had realized the need to challenge the popular notions of people about God.

In Ormoc, the stronger element which surfaced from people's religious grasp of the situation appears to be human culpability. A relief worker remarked that people as a rule were 'putting the blame on (human beings) rather than on God with regard to the destruction of the typhoon'. The ecological issue was central in the ecumenical 'Day of Mourning'. After stating that the 'exploitation of God's creation is contrary to our faith', a prayer mentioning the need for 'respect and care for (God's) creation so that (God's) people everywhere will live happily together with the rest of (God's) creation' was said. The readings used came not only from Scripture (Gen. 1.1–31; Deut. 30.19–20; John 10.10), but also from the Pastoral Letter of the Catholic Bishops' Conference of the Philippines on ecology and the Statement of the United Church of Christ on environmental concern. The prayers after the homily were also very explicit about care for the earth.

Lord, we exploited your creation and polluted nature. We denuded forests which gave life. Trees have been lost. What we owe nature we will pay for heavily.

Lord, we violated the rights of your children. They had been ignored, deceived, suffered, humiliated, arrested. We need to persevere to obtain life in harmony with nature.

Lord, we violated your church by ignoring the needs of our brothers and sisters. We have been tempted by power and have become greedy and hungry for wealth.

Lord, through your Holy Spirit, deliver us from calamities which are of our own making. May our hearts return to You and may we live lives in solidarity with nature. Thus, we will realize our responsibility as stewards of Your creation. May we live in hope. The earth is God's and so are we. Amen.

II. Theological-pastoral reflection

In retrospect, we see that the search for and care of survivors had rightly been given priority in the two natural disasters. Rescue operations had to be undertaken, the hurt had to be cared for, those shocked and bereaved had to be comforted, the hungry and the thirsty had to be given provisions, those rendered homeless had to be sheltered, and the dead had to be buried for the sake of the living. Such active concern for life takes precedence over theological reflection. The Buddha's illustration for dealing with emergencies is apropos here.[3] A person pierced by a poisoned arrow does not reflect on what the arrow which has pierced his body can possibly mean. What this person must do at once is to remove the arrow lest his whole body be poisoned.

But critical theological reflection must follow if the gospel is to leaven the experience. Obviously influenced by the presuppositions of the Filipino cultural world-view, the image of God as sovereign and powerful, whose will is equated with what happens in the world, still as a rule holds sway over Filipino minds. Coupled with the cultural perception that human beings are naturally weak, the images of all-powerful God and helpless creature mutually reinforce and legitimate each other. Such perception easily undermines human initiative and obscures human responsibility. It also wrongly blames God for the calamities which befall human communities.

Instead of introducing an extraneous element to purify such understanding, it is pastorally advantageous to discern and build in a positive cultural element. In this case, we find in the culture itself a belief that while it is God who manifests life-giving goodness and kindness, people remain responsible for the situations they find themselves in. In the words of a Filipino proverb, '*Nasa Diyos ang awa, nasa tao ang gawa*' ('Loving kindness on God's part; effort on the part of human beings'). This belief, together with the growing consciousness of human responsibility for the natural environment, can, perhaps, begin to change the earlier cultural presuppositions about God.

For Christians, moreover, the life-giving thrust of their culture is fostered through the humanizing influence of the Gospel. The conviction that God, though powerful, is not an autocrat but rather a loving God whose will and action are directed towards what gives life, rather than towards suffering and death, challenges the cultural perception that God punishes and brings destruction to call people to repentance.

Finally, the two disasters, from the perspective of evangelization, were teachable moments. They could have been exceptional opportunities to purify the negative Fillipino understanding about God and the divine will. But this specifically religious dimension was, for the larger part, unattended to, whether in liturgical celebrations or critical theological reflection. The efforts to address this issue were far too few. It is indeed regrettable that such opportune moments to instruct most meaningfully and compellingly had been missed.

Notes

1. J. M. de Mesa, *And God Said, 'Bahala Na!': The Theme of Providence in the Lowland Filipino Context*, Quezon City 1979, 81–92.

2. *Catechism of the Council of Trent for Parish Priests*, New York 1934, 583.

3. *The Teaching of Buddha*, Tokyo 1966, 296–8.

New Rituals through AIDS

Jan Ruijter

In the middle of 1991, in the Moses and Aaron church in the heart of Amsterdam, which by dedication is Catholic, the funeral was 'celebrated' of Danja Macaré, who had died of AIDS at an early age. After the event, the undertaker remarked, 'That was not a traditional church service, but it was an intensely religious event.' I had the privilege of taking the funeral, and said that Danja Macaré was safe with us: her body lay amongst us as though it were in a large living room at home, with her own decor of photographs and pictures from her childhood, and a half-knitted jumper as a symbol of her incomplete life. Both her mother and her grandmother spoke. Six months earlier Danja, already seriously ill, had had a deep conversation with Queen Beatrix, who was present at the ceremonial reopening of the restored church building. Danja had presented flowers to her; the queen had accepted them with a warm handshake, and had gone into the church with her hand on Danya's shoulder.

AIDS education

Among other things, the Moses and Aaron church is used as the hall for the adjoining Moses House, an adult education centre. In that house and in the church, for five years we have already held in-depth meetings with people infected with the HIV virus (those who have, or are likely to get, AIDS), with (ex)-drug users, their partners and members of their families, doctors, nurses, buddies, ethicists, pastors, psychologists, policy-makers, and so on. The meetings are also attended by representatives of The Rainbow, the inter-church foundation for aid to drug users; the Schorer Foundation; the Consultation Bureau for Homosexuals; the National Commission for Combating AIDS; and the Dutch HIV Association.

We began our sessions for providing information and holding dialogues five years after the first AIDS case had been registered in the Netherlands, in 1982. Initially, we gave priority to medical-technical, psychological and social education, in which those who were HIV positive or had AIDS themselves did the lion's share of the work. It was striking that people from very different backgrounds – church members and the unchurched, agnostics and atheists, members of the Salvation Army, homosexuals and clergy, prostitutes and the cream of the nation – listened to one another with open minds and hearts, indeed with respect, love and mutual trust. Hardly a discordant note was heard. These encounters were a notable plea against anxiety and discrimination.

After the first series of meetings, each attended by about a hundred people, we had to dig even deeper. There was an increasing need for more background information; the question of AIDS and the ending of life in particular remained a burning one. We explored this theme along with the AIDS Task Group of the Amsterdam Council of Churches, and now went on to discuss possible forms of the active ending of life just as openly and as urgently as we had previously discussed other subjects associated with AIDS. Apart from suicide, the wish for euthanasia on the part of some people with AIDS was specifically put on the agenda. Was there a plea for euthanasia? No; rather, there was great hesitation, though some people thought that one should not refuse this last cup of cold water to people who were genuinely asking for it. But precisely by making it possible to discuss these things, by talking about them together as intensively as we did, people became more cautious than they had been previously. In the Netherlands there is no question of irresponsible action, either in hospitals with specialists or at home with local doctors and the family. In contrast to what has sometimes been claimed abroad, people are very cautious and very scrupulous about euthanasia. And they have become even more careful as a result of discussions like those in the Moses House, with all the emotions involved.

Farewell to life

Almost automatically, a new theme then emerged: saying good-bye, the funeral and the mourning for people who are often young. AIDS seems to be prompting a catching-up process around an increasing number of tabus of our time: looking after the seriously ill, being with the dying, also in possible cases of suicide and euthanasia, and mourning.

So our information days developed into a triptych. The introductions and discussions of past years have been printed in five booklets, thousands of which have been circulated.[1]

One striking fact is that in the information-giving and discussion about AIDS, the primacy has increasingly shifted from what 'experts' have to say to the experiences of people with AIDS as expressed by the individuals concerned. Their stories need not be supported or endorsed by the reflections of, for example, doctors, psychologists, ethicists and pastors. The deepest of the experiences related by people with AIDS are so important and so powerful that they legitimate themselves. The people with AIDS are themselves the 'experts', their stories are authentic, what they say and want does not need to be justified by third parties, and they do not even need the insights of official *periti* who are present. And the same goes for what buddies, partners and members of the family say about the people with AIDS in these meetings. Those involved learn from one another, and themselves define what form the last part of the life of people with AIDS will take.

That also applies particularly to saying farewell to life. Old, worn-out and indeed stale rituals before and after death give place to creative, spontaneous and touching forms of bidding farewell and of mutual support for the dying and those who are left behind, certainly when young people with AIDS are the ones who die. Then parents and friends want to demonstrate their involvement both before and after the death. It is clear that people can live life with dignity to the end only if they are surrounded with a throng of those whom they love most and who care most for them. Together these form a close company to strengthen and support, to provide care and encouragement, and afterwards to remember. What is better than that the hand which you hold when you bid your final farewell has caressed you and changed your linen? And what is better than that the mouth which says the last words of farewell to you has kissed you?

On various occasions Ria Bos, the mother of Marieke, who died of AIDS at an early age, told in the Moses House how her daughter had arranged the farewell and the funeral beforehand with those who were closest to her. Sometimes the undertaker is open to the wishes of the person involved. With Marieke that was not the case. Then she resolved to arrange everything herself. Have a coffin made. Arrange who would carry the coffin. Hire cars. Design cards and have them printed. Marieke wanted her body to lie at home, and asked for the coffin to be made warm and attractive and lined with fleecy material and red satin. She also wanted everyone to write his or her name on a white card; all the cards were to be put inside the lid before the coffin was closed. Marieke also made arrangements with the discotheque 'Dansen bij Jansen' in the centre of Amsterdam. After the funeral, anyone could go there: it was all right for them to be a bit sad about

Marieke, but on the day of the funeral above all they were not to go and sit moping at home. Ria Bos bore witness that this period was very important: 'So everyone shared the way to the last farewell. In the week before her death, with great regularity the door would shut behind Marieke and someone else. And they would say good-bye. Marieke was ready to die. She was able to arrange everything herself. And she could say "Good-bye" to those whom she loved. Marieke's funeral, as the conclusion of this period, could almost be called a festal occasion. Under her organization.'

In the Moses House, Jan Christiaan Haye as a buddy told about the funeral of one of his clients who, true to style, had made the end of his life a baroque performance. The funeral was the last act which he himself had also arranged: 'A splendid ancient hearse drawn by four horses with black capes, and muffled hoofs, went at walking pace through Amsterdam for an hour.'

Tineke van der Kruk, a nurse who works in the AIDS unit of the great Amsterdam AMC hospital, also told in the Moses House how a new culture is coming into being at dying and at funerals, or rather how people are going back to what used to be the custom. She indicated that people often prefer to stay at home when they come closer to dying; this increasingly becomes possible with the support of professional help. People want to take their funerals into their own hands. Here is a quotation from her introduction. 'Young people above all, especially those with AIDS, have perplexed the undertakers greatly. For these often somewhat elderly men it must have been shocking, to say the least, to talk to people with AIDS about the colour of the coffin: yellow or white, colours which were not available earlier. Not to mention the lively funerals via the Amstel, burials by boat; with an embarcation at the Berlage Bridge and disembarcation at the Zorgvlied Cemetery. And helpers have got goose-pimples hearing what a splendid spot was found at Zorgvlied and what piece of music proved most suitable, on closer inspection, to play at the lowering of the coffin.'

At one of the most recent discussions in the Moses House Willem Bode, who had come to the terminal phase of AIDS, said that he wanted to be cremated. Then his ashes were to be kept in a columbarium. He wanted to have the urn covered with little mirrors, so that those who thought of him were reflected by him: a realization of the age-old *memento mori* which he himself had invented in this modern time. One of the regular speakers at the AIDS conferences in the Moses House is Fr Jan van Kilsdonk SJ. His personal style of ministry includes being with the dying, including many young people who are suffering from AIDS. He has repeatedly recalled that only when the dying person asks spontaneously and innocently for sacramental anointing does he perform this. He also bore witness that he has never encountered guilt feelings in the young people with AIDS whom he has supported: 'By nature, from within, the homosexual person has no feeling of guilt. Not even those who are afflicted with AIDS. The sick person experiences AIDS as a completely undeserved fate.' He has also stood dozens of times at the graves or at the cremations of girls or boys who – as he put it – 'had begun to hate the light of life and had themselves opened the door of death, often very violently'. And he went on: 'We always said farewell to him or her as someone who had suffered more than we had and had thus become more admirable, perhaps more majestic.'

In the course of the past five years I have often been at the funerals of people who died of AIDS and kept them company as they were dying, people who had joined in the information sessions and discussions at the Moses House. They had become friends: Paul, Ivo, Martin, Danja, Bertus, John and Kees. When I spoke at the funerals, usually in a crematorium, I tried to express the spirit of the dead person's life. Because most of them had given much in the last phase of their lives they had also gained much, in attention and love. That also radiated at their funerals. I always referred to this attention and love.

Only when the dead person had himself or herself shown some religious feeling before dying did I touch on that subject, saying just a word about it. Perhaps it is appropriate to quote the conclusion of what I said at one of these funerals: 'When we spoke about what we have come here together for now, Martin asked that we should sing "Amazing Grace", and with great fervour, because he was intensely grateful to each of us for friendship, love and care. He experienced, saw and felt you right to the end. And you stayed there with him, all day long, when his coffin lay at home, with his music, his flowers, with one another . . . it was marvellous. And now his ship is going over the sea, over the horizon, miles to go before I sleep. The way sinks over the horizon, out of sight. Or does it go further on the other side? In any case, farewell, dearest Martin.'

At Ivo's funeral, in a particularly moving way, at the end of the assembly in the crematorium the members of his family and friends gathered round the coffin, held hands and raised them high as they danced to the music. Some felt that this was a symbolic gesture which expressed the idea of the resurrection.

New rituals

At the beginning of this article I used the example of Danja Macaré's funeral in the Moses and Aaron church. Before that, I had never thought that people with AIDS who had shared in our information sessions would have wanted to hold a funeral from our church, since they were non-churchgoers. And they also chose their own songs and music which often had never resounded in a church. Beforehand we had discussed with them and the family who should speak. It was often agreed whether parts of the dead person's life should be spoken about and how, and how a greeting with flowers should be arranged. Sometimes there is need for a word of blessing, sometimes there is no question of this and the name of God is not mentioned at a funeral at the foot of the altar of the Moses and Aaron church. But Danja Macaré's funeral had such content that the Catholic broadcasting company covered it on TV and is planning to make a further programme about new rituals.

About six months after Danja Macaré's death, at the beginning of February 1992, the funeral was held in our church of Henk Koers, who died of AIDS in early middle age. He had lived a life in which much had happened that is forbidden by God and the law: poncing, stealing, organizing dog-fights, dealing in drugs – he wrote all about this himself in a lengthy biography. But at the last he experienced the deepening of life which AIDS can bring.

Before his death Henk tried to set his unfinished business in order as far as possible; he also wanted to have his own hand in his farewell. I can still see his eyes glistening when I said that it was certainly possible for his funeral to be held in our church. He too chose the songs to be played. Like Danja Macaré, he wanted Erik Windhorst – who is himself infected with the HIV virus – to go round the bier with his bagpipes. The lingering, high music of this instrument thus as it were replaced the holy water and the incense of the usual Catholic funeral, and made just as much of an impression. Henk had also arranged that forty-two red and white roses, one for each year of his life, should be given out, the white ones to good friends, the red to the loved ones who had been closest to him. These friends brought the roses up to the bier one by one and put them in a vase. Later, in the cemetery, they were again put one by one on the coffin, which was carried to the grave by Henk's family, friends and buddies. After the funeral Henk's brother Jaap said that he wanted to take over the torch and as next of kin to join in the next series of discussion days about AIDS in the Moses House. So it is remarkable how such a life is being continued after death, in others.

Dying and flowers. That makes me think of a remarkable initiative which I found in the United States. In 1990 I visited San Francisco for the international AIDS conference there. In the General Hospital I shared in a new approach. We stood in the hospital garden. Part of it had been dug up, replanted, and dedicated to people who had spent their last days in the hospital. Not much was said, and just one song was sung. The important thing was that everyone involved had a plaque on a stick with the name of a loved one on it. First the person carrying the plaque spoke into a microphone the name of the person on the plaque; then everyone said 'present' (i.e. 'he or she is present among us'); after that the plaque was put by a plant or shrub. This created a kind of garden with people's names on it. Their lives may have been broken off, but their memories are kept alive as these plants grow and blossom. A striking number of people at this gathering were from the AIDS unit and the AIDS clinic in the hospital.

Lenie van Rijendam-beek, a liberal Reformed minister in Amsterdam, was also a regular speaker on the AIDS days. She, too, was opposed to the often gruesome and impersonal standard funeral. She argued that a funeral should be stylish and should be connected with the personal life and convictions of the dead person. In her view this should determine the character of the parting. If there were differences of opinion between the sick person and those close to him or her before the death, in her view the wishes of the dead person should have priority.

She told how she and other members of the Amsterdam Council of Churches and the Humanist Association involved in these things have taken the initiative in trying to put themselves at the disposal of churches in Amsterdam and the suburbs and of training centres to help people who want to arrange a funeral their own way, without involving undertakers. These churches and other bodies were to be hospitable and give a free hand to those involved. If the ceremony takes place in church it is possible to involve the church ministers, but this need not be the case.

I recall how almost twenty years ago Leni Reijendam and I fought to keep the organ in the Westerveld crematorium. At that time people wanted to do away with it because the crematorium officials did not like the slipshod way in which children and friends of the dead played the organ and kept making mistakes: they thought that a tape recording would be much more attractive. But we saved the organ.

So increasingly, new rituals and initiatives for funerals and commemorations are coming into being, especially among homosexuals who suffer and die from AIDS. The song which is regularly sung at these funerals is not *In Paradisum*, far less *Dies Irae*, but 'Amazing Grace'. Yet more new customs have come into being in the meanwhile, not only from the American homosexual world from which the first and later many cases of AIDS occurred, but also in the Netherlands. For example, there is the annual international Memorial Day, on which those members of the family and friends who have died from AIDS are remembered, with lights and torches, with the reading out of the names of the deceased, with the singing of 'Amazing Grace', with the release of balloons and the displaying of quilts. Memorial Day is also celebrated in various places in Amsterdam: in the Old Church, the New Church, on the Dam and in the Beurs.

The phenomenon of quilts has definitively also penetrated the Netherlands. In origin the quilt is a stitched coverlet, but in the homosexual world this term is used for a cloth, a flag, on which the name and sometimes something of the experiences of a dead AIDS sufferer are put. These name-flags or memorial cloths originated in America, to put some pressure on the politicians. People used the quilts to show in a human, personal way what AIDS was really about. In America more than 20,000 of these splendidly embroidered and stitched quilts have been made; some of them have even been displayed in front of the White House. These quilts made a great impression in America, also on the politicians and on the scientists who are often concerned only with graphs and figures. The Netherlands HIV Association encourages the making of quilts, at least if those close to the dead person want it. It has proved that they are comforting reminders of the dead. In a sense a quilt brings someone to life again. Is that not a good way of mourning?

Conclusion

Death is the last birth. Death is like life. Death is rising again, living on. Certainly in friends and loved ones. That is symbolized in rituals, in liturgy. It is the service of the community, in which continuity and bonds between death and life are realized. AIDS, which affects many young people has produced new rituals, personal 'liturgies'. People are again discovering how important rituals are, how they can bring people together, channel emotions; how they put us in a position to express feelings of togetherness. Heleen Riper, who is engaged in making a survey of changes in thought about dying and death in the Netherlands, under the title *A Living Language for Death*, has expressed this clearly in an introduction in the Moses House. She rightly says: 'Rituals sometimes put us in a position to say or express things for which we have no individual words.' Rituals are sheet anchors in human life, to support and comfort the dying and to help close ones mourn. Just as the old church liturgy centred on the dead put and still puts people above themselves and their fate, so too do the new rituals which have been encouraged by the vicious AIDS epidemic in an unexpected and fortunate way. Through these rituals people transcend their fate, transcend themselves.

Translated by John Bowden

Notes

1. *Leven met Aids*, Rainbow pocketbooks, Martin Muntinga, Amsterdam 1989, ISBN 90 6766 065 5; *AIDS en Levensbëendiging*, 1990, ISBN 90 73816 03 3; *AIDS op leven en dood*, 1991, ISBN 90 73816 05 X; *Toekomst met AIDS*, ISBN 90 73816 08 4; *Future with Aids*, ISBN 90 73816 09 2 (all published by the Amsterdam Council of Churches and Moses House).

II · Traditional Responses and Questions to the Tradition

The Reaction of the Citizens of La Seu d'Urgell to the Black Death

Albert Villaró

I. The plague

Between 1347 and 1352 an epidemic caused by the bacillus *Yersinia pestis* reduced the population of Europe by a third. A series of natural catastrophes (torrential rain, floods, earthquakes) which followed one another around 1330 led to the bacillus – to be found in the respiratory organs of fleas parasitic on wild rodents on the steppes of Asia – infecting domestic rodents, especially the black rat (*Rattus rattus*).[1]

After a period of expansion through unknown parts of Asia, the disease arrived in Constantinople at the end of the summer of 1347; it was brought by a Genoan ship which had escaped from a siege laid by the Mongols to a Genoan trading post on the Crimean peninsula. The besieging forces, smitten by the plague, catapulted their dead into the city, thus infecting the Genoans inside.

From Constantinople the plague spread like lightning. The disease arrived at the seaports, and from there it advanced into the interior, going up the river valley. The appearance of the plague was preceded by great mortality among the rats. When the rats died, the fleas on them which harboured the bacillus that caused the disease attacked human beings. Bubonic plague (one of the three varieties of the disease, along with septicemia and pneumonia, and the most frequent during the plague of 1348) was not always fatal: a significant part of the population developed mild forms of the disease. This plague produced very painful inflammation of the lymphatic glands. Death took place two to three weeks after the first symptoms.

II. The city

Some recent archaeological investigations indicate that La Seu d'Urgell may have been founded by the Romans. The first mention of a bishop dates from 527, when Sant Just attended the second council of Toledo. The city became the capital of an extensive see, from which the evangelization of a large part of the Catalan Pyrenees was organized.

At the beginning of 1348, La Seu had between 1000 and 1300 inhabitants.[2] The city was waiting for the arrival of a new bishop. The last one had been Pere de Narbona, who certainly died around the end of 1347. Gillem Campoci, his successor, did not arrive until after the summer.

The bishop was the lord of the city. One of his representatives, the *veguer*, administered justice as his delegate. A second power, that of the canons, controlled worship in the cathedral and exercised direct power over much of the population of the region. A third political force, the municipality – represented by the regime of the *consolat*, which was just beginning – was trying to define itself and take its place in a system within which the divergent forces were not always balanced.

The population of La Seu was mainly engaged in agriculture: the rivers Segre and Valira flow across a fertile plain. Another important group was made up of the craftsmen who produced material which was used by the peasant population of the mountain region. A third sector which was very important for the economy was that of the wool merchants and wool producers, a civic élite which controlled the organs of municipal government.

The presence of the church was evident in many aspects of everyday life, first of all through the presence of the cathedral, an enormous twelfth-century building on which was concentrated the activity of the almost forty canons and around a hundred other clergy. The Dominicans were also intensely active; they had been installed in a priory close to the walls of the city since 1273, and could count on the unconditional support of the majority of the inhabitants of the city, as was demonstrated by the large financial contributions which the people of La Seu made for them to build their priory. La Seu, as the capital of a very extensive diocese, was also the scene of major administrative activity: there were notaries, attorneys, lawyers and a large number of clerks.

It is thanks to them that we can take ourselves back to 12 June 1348.

III. The plague in the city

On 12 June 1348, Elisenda, the wife of Guillem Peraga, went to the notary Pere d'Altarriba to make her will. On the same day Moneta de les Ribes, Guillema Palanca and the widow of Ramon Cadena also took the same action. Three wills on the same day was a quite unusual number in a city which generally registered at most between thirty and forty wills a year. This day marked the beginning of the plague. Between 12 June and 12 September the notaries in the city drafted a total of 325 wills. There was most work on 12 July: twenty wills. From then up to the middle of September the pace of dictating wills decreased.[3]

The same year saw the making of about 100 inventories, lists of goods made for the executors to comply with the conditions of the wills.[4]

Neither the wills nor any other documentation make specific reference to the deaths caused by the plague. In just two documents is there an indirect reference which shows us that the cause of the increase in the number of wills was due to the plague and not to some other cause. In the codicil of the priest Bernat Pere and in the will of Guillem Canals, both executed on 17 June and copied consecutively into the manual of the notary Pere d'Altarriba, only four of the six witnesses necessary to validate the legal act appear. As an explanation for the absence of the witnesses the copyist made reference to an *ingruente mortalitatis peste* as being responsible for the irregularity.

There is not another reference, either in the capitular acts, or in the correspondence, or in the rest of the wills, or in any later documentation. The word 'plague' never appears, despite the fact that the people of La Seu knew perfectly well of the existence of the disease and its consequences: news about the disease travelled as fast as the bacilli. From a few weeks before the middle of June there were rumours that it was on its way. A doctor in the city of Lleida (about 100 miles south of La Seu) called Jacme d'Agramont wrote a treatise on the plague, dated a few weeks before the appearance of the epidemic, on which he gave his opinion on the healthiness of the city.

> Another reason why the plague comes particularly to a city is because it is in a low-lying site with high mountains all around, and its inhabitants say that this city is a stifling place, just as Seu d'Urgell is. In a stifling place ventilation is impossible, and ventilation is something that removes putrefaction from the air.[5]

The plague certainly came from Puigcerdà, a city situated around thirty miles to the east along the river. Puigcerdà had close commercial relations with Barcelona, where the plague had appeared during the months of April and May.[6]

IV. How the citizens faced the disease

The people of La Seu give us no details about the nature of the disease which decimated them. Nevertheless, in the wills we can see a certain gradation in the way in which the testators communicate the fact that they are ill: there is clearly a difference in degree between *licet sim infirmus* and *maxima egritudine detentus*, or *iacens in maxima egritudine*, terms which certainly relate to the different stages of the disease, which developed over two weeks.

The documentation does not allow us to know with any precision the habits of the sick population. But it appears that the sick would lie in their own beds, without any kind of isolation from the other members of the family who looked after them. And if the sick person had no family, he or she would pay someone to look after them.

There were three levels to the health-care system. First were the physicians. We have hardly any references to the activity of the physician of the city, Pere Marti, who on 21 June 1348 sent for a friend in Perpignan to look after his mother. We do not have much information, and everything suggests that this was one of the first casualties of the plague. The Jewish community had its own doctor: at the beginning of the century this was Jucef De Maceres.

The surgeons were involved in eminently practical medicine. Three of them were active in La Seu during the plague: Ramon Pere, Bernat de Ribes and Ramon de Prats. At least two of them died.

The barbers were at the lowest level in the system; their job was to extract teeth, bleed and set fractures. During the summer of 1348 there was only one barber in La Seu, a certain Sorribes – we only know his name.

The three apothecaries in the city can have had little to alleviate the progress of the disease. We have the very interesting inventory of Bernat Ferrer, who also died during the plague, which gives a good indication of the medicine available at such a time: it includes many weird and wonderful substances, but they could hardly have made any mark on the plague.

V. The funeral rites

The funeral rites observed by the inhabitants of La Seu in the middle of the fourteenth century were complex, and apparently were not modified during the plague. At least the testators dictated the funeral arrangements with the confidence that these would be respected, even if the practical implementation of many of them was to be burdened by the large quantity of people who died each day.

The dead were first washed, then put into a simple linen shroud and laid in a wooden coffin. The dead person would lie in the house, lit by candles.

The majority of the funeral rites were concentrated on the burial ceremony. The procession which escorted the corpse from the house to the tomb was a ceremony full of religious significance and coloured by social status. The splendour of the funeral escort depended on the social position of the dead person.

The procession depended on the presence of priests (canons and other clergy), who were paid to be there. The coffin-bearers carried the coffin on their shoulders, reciting an obsequy as they went. However, what made the procession notable was its escort, consisting of groups of poor people, dressed specially for the occasion, and wearing veils. Their number varied between twelve and sixty, and they were chosen by the dead person's executors. It is calculated that about ten processions with the poor were organized during the two months that the epidemic lasted.

The place of burial was chosen in the will. There were nine cemeteries in La Seu and the choice of a cemetery depended on the social status of the dead or their particular devotions. The right to burial generally depended on a small financial donation which increased through the categories of places of burial chosen. The most prestigious places in La Seu were the two cloisters, those of the cathedral and the Dominican priory.

All the wills contain dispositions of a religious kind, differing in accordance with the financial resources of the testator and his or her particular devotions. Obsequies, anniversary masses, donations to church work, donations and food for the preachers – the variety was enormous and sheds light on very varied aspects of the liturgy and the religious life of the time.

VI. The consequences of the epidemic

It is difficult to say precisely how many deaths the epidemic resulted in. We have a total of 325 wills in which there are general references to the bad state of health of those making them. On the other hand, we have important groups – the Jews, the poor, the nuns, the young – who made no will and who were affected by the scourge to the same degree, if not more so. If we accept that the population of the city was 1,300, the approximate number of victims could be set at between 300 and 500, a percentage which fluctuates between twenty and thirty-five per cent of the total population.

The demographic crisis led to a very serious decline in the occupation of the region which lasted almost until the beginning of the sixteenth century as a result of further outbreaks of the plague and the bloody civil war against Juan II. The effects of this decline can be clearly seen in works like the *Spill Manifest de Totes les Coses del Vescomdat de Catellbò*, which lists all the *masos rònecs* (abandoned farmhouses) near to La Seu.[7]

The economic consequences were immediately evident. One can take the reduction to minimal level of money-lending during the months of the plague as a reliable indicator of the level of economic activity. Generally, before harvest time – which took place in the region during the end of June and throughout the month of July, in the mountain country – the peasants went to the money-lenders in order to be able to obtain the grain that they needed to live on until the proceeds of the harvest came in. In subsequent years this activity recovered, but the countryside indicated by the documents is substantially different: properties in general are listed as belonging to dead people and the descriptions of fields, vineyards and meadows are one long list of the old dead proprietors.[8]

The economic difficulties caused by the mortality lasted for a long time: King Pere el Cerimoniós exempted the neighbouring monastery of Sant Serni de Tavèrnoles and all the parishes of the diocese from the payment of tribute *propter pestilentiam vel malitiam temporis*.[9]

As for public order, the apparent serenity and lack of conflict during the months of the plague stands out all the more. Perhaps the best proof of this is the continuation of confidence in public faith shown by the sick of La Seu. Emery, in his article on the plague in Perpignan, described how the inhabitants of the capital of Roselló went to their notaries in quite a normal way:

> It is evident that a sick man or woman in the middle of the plague of 1348 in Perpignan had a reasonable chance to make public his or her last wishes. And a will, written by a professional clerk, and witnessed by a minimum of five people, represented a high level of social organization. It does not appear possible that such documents, in the quantities indicated [28 wills] could have been produced in a time of general panic and terror.[10]

Emery drew these conclusions from twenty wills preserved in Perpignan.

The relationship of wills to the population of the capital of Rosselló is of one or two wills per thousand of the population. In La Seu, just one hundred miles from Perpignan, the proportion is extraordinarily higher: two hundred and fifty wills for each thousand inhabitants. Calm there seems to have been total.

Mention of the plague as the reason why it had not proved possible to assemble the necessary witnesses could be the only exception to this tranquillity. What happened on 17 June 1348? Perhaps this was a day on which the plague showed itself in all its force: rumours became reality and the citizens were aware that the plague was attacking them directly. We do not know whether alarm and desperation spread through the population. However, this difficult moment does not seem to have lasted long. The next day the wills continued to be executed with utter normality, up to the end of the plague almost two months later.

This apparent calm contrasts with the violent disturbances which arose in the summer of 1348 in various points of Catalonia, directed against the Jewish communities. In various Catalan cities (Cervera, Tarrega, Girona, all comparable in size to La Seu), the Jews were attacked because they were thought responsible for the spread of the disease. This did not happen in La Seu: the small Jewish community was respected and even received royal support later, since in 1367 it was granted permission to build a new synagogue.[11]

In the summer of 1348 the same king, Pere el Cerimoniós, made a sad journey to escape from the plague and the rebel nobility of Aragon: his two Jewish doctors went ahead to check out the rooms to which the royal party was going. Despite these precautions, the queen died of the plague in Teruel.

VII. Conclusions

The plague lay over La Seu between June and August 1348 and killed a third of its inhabitants. In spite of that, the mortality does not seem to have affected the behaviour of the population, contrary to what happened in other parts of Europe. We have no attacks on the Jews, nor was there a massive emigration by the population to areas which were considered more secure. The legal sources are not rich in details of social behaviour, but they allow us to glimpse how the pulse of everyday life kept going.

One word might define the attitude of the city: resignation. We do not know how different La Seu was from places like Cervera, Barcelona or Florence, where public order changed considerably, with attacks on the Jews and massive emigrations of the population.

Are we to suppose that the church, an institution present in every sphere of city life, as the seat of the bishop, had a positive influence? Did the particular character of its inhabitants, mountain people, accustomed to survival in a hostile environment, determine this serene behaviour?

We do not know. In any case, the repercussions were not immediate. The consolidation of new forms of spirituality, more external and spectacular, possibly derive from the time of the plague, but they were not consolidated or defined until very much later. The plague, blind death, periodically visited the city later, but without the virulence of the epidemic of 1348. Later sources show neither lament nor any apocalyptic protests. In a few years the presence of epidemics became a normal fact, accepted by the population, which struggled against them with the best means at its disposal: shutting the city gates and preventing the entrance of people from the infected areas, generally without success.

The people of La Seu became accustomed to expect pestilence in the summer. The recollection of the first plague, the most violent and spectacular, gradually faded in popular memory.

Translated by Mortimer Bear

Notes

1. It is impossible to give a bibliography on the Black Death here. As basic works, I would simply mention P. Ziegler, *The Black Death*, London 1972; M. R. da Costa, *As pestes medievais europeias, e o Regimento proveytoso contra ha pestenença*, Fontes Documentáis Portuguesas XII, Paris 1979.

2. C. Battle, *La Seu d'Urgell medieval. La ciutat i els seus habitants*, Barcelona 1987.

3. A. Villaró, 'La pesta negra, el 1348, a la Seu d'Urgell', *Urgellia* VIII, 1987/8, 271–302.

4. A. Villaró, 'Noves dades sobre la pesta negra a la Seu (1348). Disposicions pietoses l'any de la pesta', *Urgellia* IX, 1988/9, 343–64.

5. J. Veny, *Regiment de preservació de pestilencia, de Jacme d'Agramont (segle XIV)*, Tarragona 1971, 63.

6. A. Ubieto, 'Cronologia del desarrollo la Peste Negra en la Peninsula Ibérica', *Cuadernos de Historia* V, 1971, 49.

7. P. Trago, *Spill Manifest de Totes les Coses del Vescomdat de Catellbò*, ed Cebrià Barau, La Seu d'Urgell, 1983.

8. Villaró, 'La pesta negra' (n. 3), 284.

9. A. Lopez de Meneses, *Documentos acerca de la Peste Negra en los dominios de la Corona de Aragón*, Estudios de Edad Media de la Corona de Aragón VI, CSIC, Saragossa 1950, document 128.

10. R. W. Emery, 'The Black Death of 1348 in Perpignan', *Speculum* LXII, 4, 167, 611–23.

11. Battle, *La Seu d'Urgell medieval* (n. 2), 106.

Lamentation and Mass Death

Andrés Torres Queiruga

Death cannot be assimilated by life. For the living self it represents the threat of nothingness: the negation which questions being and poses itself as the last question between human beings and God. When the death is mass death, the darkness that it brings embraces the whole horizon and settles on the community, questioning it to its roots by the impenetrable obscurity of an evil which constantly returns. Hence the need for some emotional discharge, for an effort to rediscover meaning and to search for new ways for life.

This is where mourning has its place and plays an important role. This is a role which even in our secular world usually includes recourse to religion because of the radical quality of the shock which provokes it. In any case, within believing communities such recourse comes first. Worship is then its natural place, as is evident from a long history of lamentations, petitions, processions and celebrations of a distinct kind.[1]

This history provides a wealth of actions and texts, of emotional expressions, statements of feeling and even programmes for the future. But at the same time it can be a burden which not only limits creativity but imprisons the community in out-of-date schemes, preventing it from being open to the fullness of meaning and salvation, achieved with difficulty in a history which culminates in Christ and is actualized in the constantly renewed presence of the Spirit.

A keen awareness of this ambivalence colours the basic preoccupation of the present reflections. I do not pretend to offer a model of celebration. Rather, given the basic importance of worship, I want to interpret it in the light of the image of God revealed in Christ and to show the theological conditions which must go with any specific celebration. These will not be all the conditions, but the ones which I shall analyse seem indispensable for preserving both the 'honour of God' and effective salvation for human beings.

Worship as the truth of reality

Great disturbances in particular tend to make worship most profoundly real. Directly theological language, with its 'divine words', tends to induce a sacralizing dualism which makes worship a separate area within life – *temenos, templum*, that which has been separated and cut off – not an action of life itself. Here the very secular but brilliantly profound understanding of Hegel could be of considerable help.

Hegel understood very well that worship, more than any moralizing 'chatter', represents and actualizes the real truth that faith discovers, but ordinary life tends to hide: 'The act of worship consists in participation in this reconciliation which has come about in it and for it.'[2] So the worshipping community is not an artificial or superficially symbolic entity, but makes reality and its true meaning visible: 'worship is the active process of bringing forward into reality a previously determined unity, and the enjoyment of it, so that what is potentially in faith may also be realized, felt and enjoyed' (1824, 156). To actualize the unity – 'to know myself in God as my truth and God in me' – worship actualizes 'the truth', and to do so expresses 'supreme and absolute joy' (1827, 227–8). In this way, faced with deceit, division or even the horror of outward appearances, cultic action restores the true integrity of the real as founded and saved in God. In cultic action we recognize ourselves as we truly are: sinners who know that they have been pardoned; brothers and sisters who welcome, help and share with one another; children whom the Father enables to live a life whose definitive meaning is guaranteed in the face of evil.

But Hegel is not naive and – while in any case reserving his rational optimism for philosophical reconciliation – points out that this is not an unmediated truth or a cheap cheerfulness: 'here the heart must break, that is to say, the natural will, the natural consciousness is to be relinquished' (1824, 167). The criticism of the cult as something which is a merely external objectification unless the heart is converted, that criticism which motivated the prophets and Jesus, rings out quite clearly. Furthermore, neither conversion nor realization can ever be complete: 'Above this sphere there broods a feeling of sadness which does not disappear' (1824, 165). Worship always remains open to a further fullness, a fullness that a 'we' which is not that of the Hegel but of the biblical revelation knows to correspond with eschatological promise and salvation.

Be this as it may, the stress on interiority must not mislead us about the essentially communal and historical dimension of the cult. To persist in it, treating it as Hegel does, would be truly tautological. However, it is important to remember it, since it explains the demand that cultic action should demonstrate its truth in a community which on the one hand shows itself to be reconciled, active and in solidarity, and on the other gives itself a historical context, recalling, interiorizing and actualizing a reading of the past: 'So ultimately the aim of worship is that individuals should engage in the same process and themselves be members of the community in which the Spirit is alive' (ibid.).

Clearly, what I have said does not claim to be an exercise in being strictly faithful to Hegel. Hegel, as well as being an inestimable help, is ultimately the pretext for achieving a real and true celebration. To be the determination of this truth does not require us to accept the Hegelian image of God – though without doubt we still have much to learn from this – but does require us to rely on the loving and saving personalism of the God of Jesus.

So the question is how to achieve a true celebration which allows us to experience the concrete situation in its true reality. That means experiencing it in its direct impact on the sensibility of the group, though *to the degree that* this impact is developed from the awareness which is both expressed and confessed and celebrates the presence of God in it. It is this presence that determines for the believer the ultimate meaning of what happens: it is the 'other side of the moon', which allows an integration of the vision, shattering discourse at a direct level – with its apathy or its despair, its escapism or its totalitarian reaction – to accept the integral truth, which includes the infinite profundity of its roots in God.

The anguish, the horror, the disorder of mass death are the first-fruits, the visible face which should be brought to the celebration; otherwise it will prove bloodless and lifeless. For this it must use all available expressiveness, both spontaneous and inherited, and in addition value the resources of popular mourning which are psychologically therapeutic and socially integrating,[3] or the great biblical lamentations. However, this alone is not enough. Everything has to be integrated into an experience of faith which puts in first place the fundamental datum: the living presence of God which makes it possible to restore meaning, to overcome anguish and integrate horror.

This is where the critical work begins. So the key is how this factor is introduced. Because it is invisible, its presence needs to be evoked and re-presented in its true meaning and its real truth. For the whole prophetic tradition knows of the constant danger of falsification for fear of tabu or for magical manipulation. And a theological awareness with a sense of history has to beware of any interpretation that does not do justice to the absolute self-giving of God the creator and saviour.

The wealth of language in the Bible and in worship

The caution mentioned above proves to be vital and urgent. That is because the way in which God is presented in worship defines the ultimate meaning of the celebration, opening it up to its saving efficacy or, conversely, distorting it so that it evokes alienating fantasies or encourages divergent attitudes. Moreover, this caution is necessary everywhere: since worship, to use Schleiermacher's fine expression, is a 'representative action', all its elements define the 'great syntagma of the celebration':[4] word and action, time and space, disposition and rhythm. Nevertheless, we shall centre on the word, because its determinative role cannot be ignored: as the Council says of revelation, the other elements give depth to the word, but it is the word which definitively illuminates them and explains 'their mystery' (cf. *Dei Verbum* 2). To a decisive extent the whole meaning of the celebration depends on what is said in it.

There is no need today to stress that this emphasis in no way amounts to an abstract intellectualism. Awareness of the many dimensions of language has long since been achieved. And above all as a result of the revaluation of ordinary language by the later Wittgenstein, the pragmatic dimension has taken on enormous importance. There is no going back on J. L. Austin's stress that words are not only 'locutionary acts' which express objective acts but are also 'illocutionary acts' which 'do things' and indeed 'perlocutionary acts' which transform 'the feelings, thoughts and actions of the hearer, the speaker, or others'.[5] Since his work, and that of J. Searle,[6] these ideas have simply been confirmed, amplified and deepened. To this must be added the renewed emphasis on the symbolic, which is definitively no longer conceived of as a primitive, infantile or capricious character-ization, but is seen as a specific and irreducible use of language. With the great riches of its twofold stratification of meaning, it makes it possible to express the inexpressible; and with its 'ontological vehemence' it opens up new dimensions in the exploration of reality.[7]

All this has an immediate application in the sphere of religious language, which in many ways is a privileged one. This is not only because, now that the one-dimensional character of positivism has been overcome, the legitimacy of this language has been recognized,[8] but above all because it has proved more possible to explore and exploit its specific riches, which were formerly hidden too much by an excessive reduction to a merely objective reference. The new conception of the symbolic allows us to see that the references of religious language are to the infinite horizon of Transcendence. And the new pragmatic awareness has put in first place the role of religious language in expression and realization, its capacity to involve and transform the speaker to the very depths.[9]

In this way it is clear that language not only constitutes the fundamental medium of revelation – as the theological tradition has always seen – but that it shapes and structures the life of worship to the very depths. Indeed liturgical renewal has taken account of this by putting special emphasis on use of the enormous expressive potential contained in scripture. Read properly, the basic texts open out all the register of their mythical and symbolic content and give spoken expression to all the great feelings which can provide an opening to the saving presence of the Lord.

To be specific, the book of Lamentations, a great many Psalms and various hymns and expressions in the Bible are splendid material for authentic worship in the face of the threat of pain, misfortune and death. The cultivation of sensitivity, apprenticeship in prayer, the recovery of historical memory, availability before God, find their best nourishment here, constituting an indispensable model and aid by which the community of the faithful can rediscover meaning, live out its hope and find a basis for its action.

'False talk infects the soul'

Nevertheless, not everything is simple and straightforward. Attention to the pragmatic, perhaps as a natural compensatory tendency, has not come about without tension with the strictly cognitive and therefore the ontological value and the truth in religious language: the distinction made in Oxford between a left (non-cognitive) and a right (cognitive) is a good test. If there is a spontaneous tendency to sacralize biblical language, without effective attention to its historicity (which in theory is now generally accepted), it runs the risk of using texts or expressions which convey an image that is not totally that of the God of Jesus. And in the sensitive sphere of lamentation and prayer in the face of evil in its most tremendous and catastrophic forms, this image can have very harmful effects.

I am thinking above all of the divine image present in so many Old Testament texts, of a particular way in which they describe evil. God is presented as its direct cause, negatively not seeking to avoid it, and positively sending it as a punishment or even using it as a demonstration of his wrath or his vengeance. The text of Lamentations, which is magnificent in so many aspects, proves horribly paradigmatic in this respect: 'without mercy', 'in his wrath', 'like a flaming fire', 'like an enemy

(Lam. 2.2–6).[10] And in general the words of Xavier Léon-Dufour still continue to be valid: 'The Israelite tradition never abandoned the bold principle formulated by Amos: "Does evil befall a city, unless the Lord has done it?" (Amos 3.6; cf. Ex. 8.12–28; Isa. 7.18). However, this intransigence provoked tremendous reactions: "There is no God!" (Ps. 10.4; 14.1), conclude the wicked when faced with the evil of the world, or only a God "incapable of knowledge" (73.11); so Job's wife consistently calls on her husband to "Curse God!" (Job 29).'[11]

To ignore this would be suicidal. To adopt the typical strategy of resorting to partial accommodations when the time has come for a 'paradigm change'[12] would not be a good strategy. Because nobody claims to deny the evident value of these texts: not only their *expressive* but also their positive *historical function*, in that such texts were – at that point – the means of being able to confess the lordship of God despite an inadequate categorization of the autonomy of the creature, to proclaim his justice from the Deuteronomic doctrine of retribution, or, as we can read in Lamentations and so many Psalms, to continue to put all one's trust in the Lord. *Today*, however, the historical progress of revelation allows us, indeed requires us, to keep what has been achieved without going on to pay the terrible prices for it. The God of Jesus does not send evil without suffering with us; does not punish without pardoning unconditionally; does not become angry without 'love', in other words without *consisting* solely in loving.[13] (And in revealing this Jesus does not deny the Old Testament, but corrects it and 'fulfils it' with respect to what is there in embryonic form and comes to be expressed in its best texts.)

To lament mass death in Christian worship and confront the terrible face of history cannot consist in 'asking' God why he sends the disaster or why he is angry with us, because he certainly is not; far less can it consist in 'rebuking' him as though he were the guilty one or even 'asking' him to ward it off, as though he were the one responsible; or to 'punish' malefactors as if he were the empirical substitution for our justice. To retain out of repetitive inertia the expressions which convey these false assumptions might seem faithfulness to the letter – or even 'elegant' theological rhetoric – but in fact it represents profound infidelity to the living Word and is a very grave responsibility as far as faith is concerned.

It should not be necessary to emphasize the objective wealth contained in any expression of ordinary language[14] or its power to shape the mind before subjective judgment, and with far more force than such judgment. The mind is shaped solely by means of language: it acts in it and moulds its innermost depths by it. A false expression necessarily perverts this mediation, damaging its development. Socrates expressed this in a splendid way, specifically in connection with death: 'You should know, excellent Crito, that false words are not only evil in themselves, but they infect the soul with evil soul' (*Phaedo* 115e).

When dealing with a language as strongly perlocutionary as religious language and on the decisive point of the very image of God, it is clear that we are touching on the very roots of the spirit. This is all the more the case in a celebration which is completely structured in a way which is to make the word effective. Objectively, given the invisibility of God, the verbal icon constitutes the very condition of his presence to the consciousness and also determines the way in which it is perceived.[15] Subjectively, the whole tradition insists, rightly, that the participants should let themselves be shaped by the word proclaimed: *mens nostra concordet voci nostrae*, 'may our mind agree with our voices', as the Benedictine rule puts it.[16]

In the face of such objective efficacy it is illegitimate to put exclusive stress on the *subjective intention*, saying that one does not pretend to 'blame' God, or to shield oneself by *expressive values*, asserting that all one is doing is seeking to express human sadness or dependency before God: these values are real, but they cannot be absolutized when they clash with the value of truth which language also aims to reflect (a blasphemy can be an effective expressive means of giving great perlocutionary force to a threat, but the objective truth of its words requires that it should not be uttered). Independently of any kind of subjectivity, 'the word implies who I am for you and who you are for me'.[17] In this case this 'you' is nothing less than God, and we cannot ever forget the Barthian warning that 'God is God and man is man'. It is the supreme norm which decides the ultimate truth of the situation, and the truth of our expression should also decide that.

To attend to this demand by modifying language, using or critically transforming the word of scripture – selecting it and re-reading it in the light of Christ – seeking new texts both in the other religions or in the great 'poets' (to use Heidegger's term) and creating new ones when necessary, can sometimes prove difficult and even very hard. But it certainly purifies worship (testing to see whether it is true that our prayers are full of routine topics and implications which are offensive for the honour of God: do we 'report' what happens, try to 'convince' him to be kind and take pity on our suffering, and, if necessary, offer him things in exchange?). And above all, it is truly saving; we de-centre ourselves towards God and are converted; and to die to our own particularity, as Hegel advises us, is precisely the way of arriving at our radical truth. Only on that basis can there be authentic, integrating and renewing celebration.[18]

Celebrating salvation

Since God is the ultimate reality who underlies every situation and the symbolic centre who definitively organizes celebration, it is no exaggeration to say that if we succeed in invoking God properly, it is easier to set everything in the truth.

In the first place, there is a basis through which the celebration orientates itself on living and effective solidarity. That is, provided that we have avoided what Paul Ricoeur rightly calls the 'rotten points' of religion,[19] accusation and consolation: accusation coming from God, the terrible or angry father who 'punishes'; or on the contrary the false consolation of the miraculous God who intervenes in the world by crushing the enemy, warding off the plague or raining down manna. And it is the harsh requirement of the masters of suspicion that this should be converted into cultural objectivity, extending to the same mass culture; for the same reason they stipulate that it cannot be fought with good intentions. It is necessary to accept this challenge, honestly criticizing our fantasies in order to recover the truth that they distort. We shall have taken a great step forward if we succeed in making the words of celebration evoke the presence of the God who has surrendered everything in his love and who, respecting the laws of the creature and the limits of history, shares in our being and our actions, accompanying us, giving hope and fighting on our side against evil.

So the orientation of the liturgical assembly must change radically. The expression of grief will remain and can make use of the immense riches of biblical language, but will transform it and enrich it with new contributions. Worship cannot be used to 'inform' God or to 'complain' about being forsaken; on the contrary, it must bring about awareness that our suffering is accompanied by his love and temper the legitimate expression of sorrow by confidence in his presence, avoiding a lapse into despair. Prayer does not have the sense of 'persuading God', but on the contrary of *letting ourselves be convinced* by God, by being attuned to his grief for his afflicted children and opening ourselves to his one 'commandment': that we should allow his active love to pass through ours, converting it into indignant protest, effective aid or efficient prevention of new catastrophes.

However, it is not just a matter of practical efficiency. The other dimensions can also find fitting expression. I shall mention two points.

From the poem of Gilgamesh onwards the anguish of 'everything perishes' has resounded in humanity, the inextinguishable sadness of fatal mortality which has an echo in the dark, bloodless and desolate abandonment of the biblical Sheol. However, the God of Jesus, who 'is not a

God of the dead, but of the living' (Mark 12.27; Matt. 22.32), illuminates this darkness with the certain glory of the defeat of death and of the resurrection which has now opened up in history. It is possible to polarize all the texts round this, choosing from the Old Testament those which announce life now without final defeat (Ps. 73, Daniel, II Maccabees, Wisdom), and we can proclaim the new *agalliasis*, the inextinguishable joy which now proclaims 'Happy are those who suffer', and which the Apocalypse reveals as a destiny 'with no more death, nor crying' (21.4); as a city 'without any darkness, since the glory of God is its light and its lamp is the Lamb' (21.23).

The other great sadness, that of broken communion and irreparable absence, also finds a way towards the light; it is that incurable wound which an Aztec poem expresses with a powerful exclamation:

'Shall I perhaps see them?
See my father and mother?
Will they come to give me their song and word?
No one remains with us,
We are left orphans on the earth.'[20]

Certainly, faith knows it: knows that we shall see and that we will not be left orphans (John 14.17). And it would be no bad thing if the Christian celebration of death – which is essentially a gathering focussed on 'he was dead and now is risen' and brings us together before his lifegiving gaze – had a change of emphasis. Here too it is unhealthy to spend time 'persuading' God – the only One who is 'good' (Matt. 19.17; Mark 10.18; Luke 18.19)! – to look kindly on the dead and shorten his 'punishment'. Let us take the opportunity to sing of our confidence in his salvation and to affirm communion with the dead, living out our belief in eternal life: that our dead – also and above all those who were sacrificed on the terrible altars of historical injustice – are alive in the Risen One and from him, with him, and in him, hear us and see us, enfold us in their love and guide us to life and hope.

In a century which has seen two world wars, a gulag and a Holocaust, which contemplates the slow death of the Palestinian people and the hunger of so many millions of Africans, along with the fall of the Communist dream . . . it is still necessary to celebrate. For us, that calls for courage; for the victims, that calls for hope: for God, that requires our hands and our solidarity in the painful birth of his new creation, until finally he is 'all in all' (I Cor. 15.28).

Translated by Mortimer Bear

Notes

1. The integration of the secular and the religious has not always been easy or clear, cf. P. Ariès, *L'homme devant sa mort*, Paris 1977, chs. 3–4.

2. *Vorlesungen über die Philosophie der Religion, Teil I. Einleitung: Der Begriff der Religion*, ed. W. Jaeschke, Hamburg 1983, p. 234 of the 1824 lecture (I cite the year of the lecture and the MS page, which are in the various translations).

3. In addition to the pioneering work by S. Freud, *Mourning and Melancholia* (1917), in The Penguin Freud Library XI, Harmondsworth 1984; cf. G. Gorer, *Death, Grief and Mourning*, London 1965.

4. L. A. Houssiau, 'La liturgia', in *Iniciación práctica a la Teología. 5 Etica y Práctica*, Madrid 1986, 371–3.

5. J. L. Austin, *How to do Things with Words*, Oxford 1955; cf. id., 'Religious Commitment and the Logical Status of Doctrines', *Religious Studies* 9, 1973, 39–48.

6. J. Searle, *Speech Acts. An Essay in the Philosophy of Language*, Cambridge 1969.

7. The expression comes from P. Ricoeur, who of course has devoted a number of very illuminating studies to the theme; cf. especially *La métaphore vive*, Paris 1975.

8. The nuances and the differences cannot conceal this fundamental fact, as is shown by the vast literature on the matter; cf. the synthesis by I. U. Dalferth, *Analytische Religionsphilosophie*, and A. Halder, K. Kienzler and J. Moeller, *Religionsphilosophie heute*, Düsseldorf 1988.

9. The work by Donald Evans, *The Logic of Self-Involvement: A Philosophical Study of Everyday Language with Special Reference to the Christian Use of Language about God as Creator*, London 1963, so intelligently developed above all by J. Ladrière, has shown the abundant wealth of this focus. Cf. especially the latter's *L'articulation du sens. I, Discours scientifique et parole de la foi*, Paris 1978, and *II, Les langages de la foi*, Paris 1984 (with bibliographies).

10. Without doubt, the commentary by G. F. Wood is correct: 'Cf. 1.13–15; 2.1–8; 2.22; 3.1–18; 3.43–46, where Yahweh appears among the enemy troops and shares their ferocity' (*The Jerome Biblical Commentary*, Garden City and London 1968, 610).

11. 'Sufrimiento', *Vocabulario de Teología Bíblica*, Barcelona 1973, 873.

12. With a variety of nuances and modifications, this notion has been generally accepted since T. S. Kuhn, *The Structure of Scientific Revolutions*, Chicago 1962.

13. For this cf. the other articles in this issue of *Concilium*. I personally have discussed the topic, trying to hold it together without diluting it, in *Recuperar la salvación*, Madrid 1979, 81–150; *Creo en Dios Padre*, Santander ²1986, 109–50; 'Mal', *Conceptos Fundamentales de Pastoral*, Madrid 1983, 594–603.

14. Cf. e.g. the analysis made by Austin of all that is implied in the simple fact of making an excuse, 'A Plea for Excuses', in *Philosophical Papers*, Oxford ²1970, 123–52.

15. 'Thus the language of faith refers as such to a reality which is given only in the language itself and which takes form only in it; moreover, it is revealed by it only to the degree that it is itself an act by which the believer accepts that of which his word speaks' (Ladrière, *L'articulation du sens* [n.9], I, 238–9).

16. *Regula* 19.7; cf. also Augustine, *Hoc versetur in corde quod profertur in ore*.

17. Houssiau, 'La liturgia' (n.4), 364.

18. All this really needs a separate and very thorough treatment, in view of the element of transcendence and its complex implications: I have tried to provide this in 'Más allá de la oración de petición', *Iglesia Viva* 152, 1991, 157–93.

19. P. Ricoeur, 'Religion, Faith, Atheism', in A. MacIntyre and P. Ricoeur, *The Religious Significance of Atheism*, New York 1969, 60.

20. A. M. Garibay, *La literatura de los Aztecas*, Mexico 1964, 69.

God at the Heart of Hell:
From Theodicy to the Word
of the Cross

Michel Deneken

'Auschwitz has happened, and it confronts us all.'' This cruel evidence has
put paid to a large number of convictions. And yet, despite the horror, the
experience of the Shoah has not led to atheism. If one looks at the emaciated
faces of the prisoners of the gulags, beginning with Solzhenitsyn, hope and
faith are not dead there either. However, an event like the Shoah summons
the theologian to scrutinize scripture and tradition with new sharpness,
keeping in mind the drama of humanity whose history most of the time
proves to be a way of suffering. The face of the Crucified Jesus then appears,
in a mysterious form of divine teaching, as the face which is closest to our
time. It is no longer the face of the 'good God', yet one can no longer accept
that God is distant: in the night and the fog there shines the face of the
suffering God, Jesus Christ. The philosophical problem of theodicy is also
more than pricked by the barbed wire of the camps; it proves inadequate for
giving an account both of the evil which is unleashed and the God who is
there. The work of theologians consists in seeking for the time in which they
live ways of responding to the imperious *fides quaerens intellectum*. Here
the task is formidable, so cruel does the experience of the twentieth century
seem with its fatal history of world wars, genocides and fratricidal struggles.

   First of all I shall try to bring out the need to go beyond the formal
question of theodicy to discover the power of the language of the cross.
Then I shall attempt to understand the meaning of the notion of the
suffering of God. Finally, I shall attempt to outline some approaches
which, beginning from the christology of pro-existence, can offer some
perspectives for our time.

I. Theodicy exhausted by the language of the cross

1. How does one speak of God after horror? One first observation is necessary: if the world had tipped over into atheism, with Jews at its head, a badly understood theodicy would have been put on trial very quickly, and for ever. If on the contrary, as was the case, Auschwitz did not represent the end of theology but made the questions put to it more radical; and if, as Moltmann notes, people did not cease to say the *Shema Yisrael* and *Our Father* in the camps, the question of God remains. Even if silence is fitting before the relics, theologians are called on to speak. Their enterprise might seem as foolish as that of Ezekiel, prophesying over the bones which he sees being covered with flesh once again. They are called on to consider the changes that brute reality forces on theological discourse. If Auschwitz has not made us atheists, it is because we have been able to respond – at least partially – to the question posed by modernity: that question is no longer 'Who is God?', but 'Where is God?' (Jüngel). The theologies of the death of God have been overtaken by the magnitude of what has been unleashed in humanity. God did *not* die in Auschwitz: that affirmation is not blasphemous, but is based on the living faith of Jews and Christians. God is not a relic which has survived the terror; God is very much alive, still celebrated, confessed today in Judaism and Christianity. So the question takes another form: what is put in question in Auschwitz is not God, but a certain type of theodicy.

2. The Leibnizian enterprise of theodicy is there in our history of philosophy and theology to illuminate the attempts, both before it and afterwards, to reconcile the experience of evil with the possibility of speaking of God and affirming God's existence. The notion of God's justice then posed for Leibniz the very question of the universe and its meaning. The misunderstanding here lies between a divine justice seen by the philosopher and the biblical notion of God's justice as defined by Paul. In Leibniz's theodicy God is the sum of all possibilities, and the gap which exists between God and human beings is that existing between the possible and the real. First of all, then, the question of theodicy implies that of humanity. Now in Auschwitz human nature was totally denied. That amounts to saying that theodicy can never be separated from anthropodicy. The tragic proof of this is provided by the Nazi enterprise to blot out the Judaeo-Christian religion from the surface of the earth. The denial of God allows the denial of humanity. So Jüngel was right in seeing the modern problem of the possibility of thinking of God as the question of

the guarantee of human beings. Who can guarantee human beings against the very negation of human beings by human beings, if not God? The Bible shows little taste for metaphysical speculations. God is the one who manifests himself and whose presence is experienced. So theology must put itself within the dynamic of revelation and the Word in order to show ways for the questioning of contemporaries. Now at Auschwitz, it is not God who has to be justified, but human beings in quest of new guarantees, incapable as they are of setting up ramparts against their barbarism from their own transcendence. The classical theodicy presupposes a conscious awareness of justice and goodness on the part of human beings; it also reveals a faith in the future and in progress – all notions which the twentieth century has shattered into pieces: human beings can destroy themselves; progress is no longer ideologized. In the face of a system of totalitarianism and concentration camps, theodicy can appear an unimportant intellectual game.

3. To paraphrase a remark of Cardinal Suenens, one can claim that theology after Auschwitz not only needs an *aggiornamento*, needs to be brought up to the present day, but must also help people caught up in the whirlwind of violence and who, like Job, cry out their 'Why?' to heaven, to experience an *annottamento*. They must be given courage to confront the night, to accept the apparent eclipse of God (M. Buber). That seems definitively outside the field of classical theodicy. Confronted with the horrors to which the twentieth century has given birth, more than ever it is the question of Job which stimulates theological reflection. So people of today must live 'with Christ in a world wrapped in the darkness of God . . . their piety will be a piety of contemplative kenosis which, in suffering, will undergo the trial of the darkness of God over the world and will emerge from it victorious'.[2] The specific Christian characteristic immediately appears: in the face of the death of the innocent, there emerges the figure of the suffering Christ. This Jesus of Nazareth, confessed as Christ and Lord, Suffering Servant and crucified Messiah, puts the very idea of God in crisis. Christian preaching rightly sets itself at the heart of the drama of the death of the innocent, who is the Son of God. Taking up a theme which was dear to Bonhoeffer, Barth argued that in the incarnation God agrees to lose so that man shall gain.[3] Involving himself in creation, God compromises, is identified with the crucified one. Auschwitz confirms the crisis of the concept of God, which began the day the Voice made itself heard to Abraham and does not cease to call on human beings to see God differently.

4. The language of the cross as Paul brought it to light is the expression of the most profound mystery of the incarnation. 'The mystery of the cross which is so despised and full of shame', as Justin wrote.[4] The language of the cross appears as the original Christian way of speaking of the encounter of the human and the divine which does not end up in myth but in humanization. The 'harsh word' of and about the cross weighs heavy. However, there is a risk in putting too much emphasis on the language of the cross, and a certain kenoticism, both Protestant and Catholic, has sometimes sunk into dolorism and reduced Easter to a kind of reparation for the injustice committed by human beings over Jesus. Some theologians have run this risk by refusing out of a sense of propriety to move too quickly from the cross to the resurrection. These theologians have felt that events like Auschwitz lead them to dwell on this death in order to see the world with the very eyes of God. However, Christian hope is just as radical a fact, and can appear just as scandalous as the cross itself. The resurrection is also a mystery of folly and scandal. The light of Easter did not obliterate the horizon of humanity. Johannine theology makes the cross an element in which humiliation and exaltation, obscuring and revealing, are held together dialectically. The figure of the Suffering Servant when applied to Jesus reconciles the two interpretations of the ʿebed YHWH, communal and individual. In the word of the cross, God shows himself as the love which renounces all that is not love in order to impose itself. God reveals himself in the event of the cross as 'being who exposes himself to what happens, because he involves himself in nothingness'.[5] Jesus 'occupies a zero point of mediation, being purely the passage from God to man and *remaining* for the rest of the time the one who, in that way, does not cease to *pass*'.[6]

How can Christians pursue their theological enterprise, confronted with the horror of the world? By recognizing that if Christ is confessed as the truth about God and human beings, he is a humiliated truth.[7] *Theologia crucis* and *theologia gloriae*, the theology of the cross and the theology of glory, no longer exclude each other, but are definitively linked in the incarnation itself. So in Jesus one can claim that God suffers.

II. The suffering of God

1. ' . . . to affirm simultaneously that God is immovable in himself and movable in the other does not satisfy the mind. God is not a sphinx, nor are human beings "solvers of riddles". Though obscure in itself, the mystery is enlightening. So it must be possible if not to understand, at least to

sense . . . that in God the future is the perfection of being, movement the perfection of immobility, change the perfection of immutability'.[8] Here F. Varillon touches on the Gordian knot of theodicy: if God suffers, as we say, since he cannot remain insensitive to human misery, God is capable of feeling. But does that not put his perfection in question? That is not just a scholastic question. All contemporary questioning in fact crystallizes around this difficulty. Is it just an analogy to say that God suffers? The reflections which marked the first Christian centuries soon concentrated on the Trinity, the relations between the three persons and their nature. Patripassianism was a real temptation: Noetus recognized only one person, so it is the Father who is born and who suffered. This heresy was rapidly swept aside because it denies the divinity of Christ and his equality of nature with the Father. On the other hand, the theopaschite controversies were to last more than six centuries and show the difficulty that the church fathers had in taking account of the death-resurrection of the Son while preserving the immutability of God. During the first centuries this conception received different welcomes, depending on theological sensibilities. The controversy reached its height in the sixth century. The formula *unus de trinitate passus est*, one of the Trinity suffered, lies at the heart of the debates. The Scythian monks wanted to adopt the formula, which at first had a cool welcome but which after correction was supported by Fulgentius of Ruspe in the name of the African bishops. Its integration into the Code of Justinian in 528 conferred a status on it which was confirmed in an edict addressed to Constantinople in 533 and ratified by Pope John II. The difficulty remains.

2. It is readily accepted today that the problem of the suffering of God is burdened with the Greek conceptualization and philosophy which the Fathers adopted. Thus there are criticisms of the very Hellenistic notion of *apatheia*, which is the mode of being of the Greek *theos*, of giving the biblical God, who is living and involved in the world, a relationless image without *pathos*, suffering and emotion. This justification needs to be qualified. First of all let us recall that the God of the Bible and consequently the God of Jesus is a God who is living and active, creator and saviour. Now this God is often put to the test by his creation, and very often has to complain about the terrible behaviour of his people, deaf to his calls and slow to convert. For example, in Ps. 78.41, 'They tested God again and again, and provoked the holy One of Israel', or again Jer. 31.20, '"Is Ephraim my dear son? Is he my darling child? For as often as I speak against him, I do remember him still. Therefore my heart yearns for him; I

will surely have mercy on him," says the Lord.' God suffers for his child. Jesus also suffers: before the tomb of his friend Lazarus he weeps; before Jerusalem he laments for the people which has not been able to discern the visitation of its God; and at Gethesemane he weeps in fulfilling the will of his Father. Would the church fathers at this point have betrayed the numerous scriptural indications of the suffering love of God and his passion for the world? Here one can share the judgment of Hans Urs von Balthasar, who rightly remarks that a scrupulous examination of the patristic literature shows the degree to which the Fathers distanced themselves from Greek *apatheia* and sought to preserve the original biblical revelation of God in Jesus Christ.[9] Ignatius of Antioch writes: 'Keep your gaze on him who is above all vicissitudes: the invisible one who for us was made visible; the impalpable, impassible one who for us was made passible; who suffered for us in every way (*ton apathe, ton di' hemas pantheon*).'[10] Melito of Sardis uses the dialectical pairing of *thnēton, athanaton*: mortal, immortal.[11] If, paradoxically, the Greek fathers speak of the divine *apatheia*, this is to affirm that the Son was incarnate and died according to the flesh and not to maintain some kind of insensitivity to human fate on the part of God. Progressively it was the notion of divine *pathos* which was to try to translate the way in which God suffers, and people held the paradox in one formula by speaking of the passion of the impassible.

3. The *unus ex trinitate passus est* can contain a possible response. However, this formulation is difficult to cope with. To be very brief, the passion is attributed to the flesh and the impassibility to the divinity. The *communicatio idiomatum* represents the appropriation by the *logos* of human suffering. No formula is perfect, and this way of talking about the suffering of the Son is not free of ambiguities. But in affirming that Jesus is true God and true man, the church admits that it is not only the man Jesus who has suffered, but also the divinity. So the question must be reversed: is there not a suffering specific to each of the persons of the Trinity? The suffering of the Father who sees his people disobeying him and turning away from him, seeing his Son handed over to the hands of the executioners; the suffering of the Son, glimpsing in night and death the will of the Father and the mysterious way of human suffering; the suffering of the Spirit which groans in the birth-pangs of the new man and the new world? Can one in fact imagine that one of the Trinity was in some way 'delegated' to confront the world without either the Father or the Spirit being involved, each according to his own mode of subsistence? Jesus risen, confessed as Christ and Lord, remains the man whose wounds are

the weft of humanity, as is revealed by the Easter encounter with Thomas. The Trinity, that community of love, lives out the vital force of the whole love of which it is the source: the vital force of the Word is the desire to communicate; it is the *amor capax verbi* (E. Jüngel);[12] and the suffering inevitable in all true love is the *caritatis est passio* (Origen).[13] To attribute passions to God has been perceived as incompatible with the perfection and the immutability which befit God. Thomas Aquinas also has cautious recourse to anthropomorphisms and when speaking, for example, of the mercy of God, stresses that this cannot be a weakness inconceivable for the deity: 'Above all is mercy to be attributed to God, nevertheless in its effect, not in the affect of feeling . . . To feel sad about another's misery is no attribute of God, but to drive it out is supremely his.'[14] Having emerged from the biblical world in which it expresses the presence of God in a passionate way in the world, anthropomorphism seems to strike fear into the theologian, who sees in it a danger of weakening the power of God or the risk of being submerged in mythology. In the face of the unleashing of evil in Auschwitz or in the gulags, the danger of taking ways which lead nowhere is no less since the real death of the people is neither analogical nor mythical. The blood of Abel still cries out.

4. The attempts at contemporary responses like those of J. Moltmann, K. Kitamori, J. Galot, D. Sölle, R. Hall, F. Varillon and G. Koch all start from the same presupposition: in the face of what has happened in this century, the way in which people have spoken of God has been seriously put in question and it is right to give the notion of God's suffering its due place. God can no longer be considered incapable of feeling, since for contemporary awareness that would be the God whom Stendhal imagined to be wicked, if he existed. That poses a formidable problem: how far is God responsible for the monstrosity of humanity when brother rages against brother? In other words, we certainly must not evade the question of knowing how one can speak of the creator, saviour, merciful God, before the charnel houses of history; however, it is not God who must be put in the dock but human beings. In this respect the theologies of the death of God are often defective. They seek to go radically, in commitment to Jesus, to the heart of human death, but want to swallow up the Father and the Spirit in it. Any assertion that God is dead can only be about the death of the Son as human being and as God, but this death is mysteriously death *in* God, as Jüngel puts it. To say it once again, God did not die in Auschwitz. He was there, mysteriously, and he remained there as the mystery of love courageously remains: 'If God loves, it is there that

he will dwell, in this position where he is vulnerable. Certainly he can only commit himself by his own free will, not as because of an intrinsic weakness. So is he God?"[5] In times of crisis, again an image forms to express God to contemporaries: at times of plague the *pietàs*, which, starting from the human experience of mothers having to carry their dead children, give a glimpse of the drama experienced by Mary with her son in solidarity with the human condition. In the twentieth century the Christs of Rouault, which look so intense and so melancholy at the same time, express an impassibility which is not indifference but a refusal to judge, a refusal to show anger. From this point of view one can affirm with Kasper that in the light of suffering and the experience of evil, the only possible response to the question of God must be both christological and staurological, in the language of the cross.[16]

5. To assert that Christ and the cross are the final revelation of the love of God, that mystery than which nothing greater can be conceived, signifies that God is limited, that God has entered into the human condition. That is the meaning of the double kenosis, that of the incarnation and that of the cross, the second being the radicalization of the first. If God shows himself as human, it is by God's demonstration of sharing the condition of humanity to the point of death. Whereas human beings use their freedom to attack their brothers and sisters and God, God uses his freedom to enter into humanity by limiting himself. Faced with Auschwitz, Judaism, too, has attempted to reflect on this limitation of God. Thus the Jewish philosopher Hans Jonas has attempted to grasp the message of Auschwitz. Rejecting any easy solution, he seeks to analyse the notion of theodicy.[17] According to him, the relationship which God institutes with the world that he has created is a passionate one.[18] By creating, God accepts suffering. In reflecting on the worldliness of God, Jonas touches on the question of his omnipotence. Here it is necessary to conceive of 'an idea of a God who, for a time – the time of the worldly future – detaches himself from any possibility of involvement in the physical process of the evolution of the world; (a God) who does not respond to the process of the evolution of his own being with a mighty hand and outstretched arm, as we Jews do each year when we remember the exodus from Egypt, but by the silent and obstinate quest for his unfulfilled goal'.[19] So God limits himself voluntarily to be present in *sym-pathy* with the world; then, having given himself totally to humankind, God has no more to give; it is then for humankind to give.[20] This self-limitation of God also has echoes in rabbinic literature. Susan Shapiro mentions a question raised by the Talmud tractate Yoma:

why did Daniel omit the word 'mighty' when, after the destruction of the First Temple, he asked about the perpetuity of the covenant (9.4ff.)? Similarly, Jeremiah omitted the word 'terrible' (32.17ff.) in speaking of God in prayer. Now the Mosaic revelation attributes four basic qualities to God: great, powerful, terrible, incorruptible (Deut.10.17). Rabbi Eleazar replies: 'Since they (Daniel and Jeremiah) knew that the Holy One, blessed be He, insists on truth, they would not ascribe false things to him.' To keep silent about one of the attributes did not seem blasphemous here, but testifies that believers have to bear witness to the truth as they experience it in their generation, taking account of a divine pedagogy.[21] In this perspective the Christian response can then be as follows: the self-limitation and renunciation of intervention in the world in the name of love for humankind is manifested by God in his Son.

III. The pro-existence of the Son: God reveals

1. Contemporary theology is ill at ease with the idea of the descent into hell. Now in the hell of humanity, whether Auschwitz or the genocide in Cambodia, if we accept the idea of a God who is mysteriously present, God can only be in that hell. If the history of religions bears witness to beliefs in deities descending into hell, Christianity alone asserts that the God who descends into hell also died and remained there.[22] The descent into hell is the paradoxical point of the solidarity and the communication of God or, more precisely, the communication is a silent abiding, invisible in the depths of the earth, and solidarity extended to all the dead since Adam. This descent is the most powerful expression of the kenosis of God. Hans Urs von Balthasar has been the most consistent in his treatment of this theme. Holy Saturday is the moment when human beings are confronted with the void. This void is the day 'when the Son is dead and when, as a result, God is inaccessible'.[23] 'The church's liturgy confronts all the disciples of the crucified Christ with this void. From the end of Good Friday to the end of Holy Saturday we must remain in the obscure silence of God . . . this void in place and time can only be looked on "from afar" (Luke 22.54) with faith by those who contemplate the dereliction of Good Friday before turning their gaze towards the rising sun of the first day.'[24] So God is in solidarity to the point of the Son's being among the dead. Eastern theology has always attributed soteriological value to this descent into hell. God is dead there, but in the dynamism of the resurrection he also draws humanity from eternal death by giving his hand to Adam. The Nazis put 'God with us' on their belt

buckles; they did not know that God-with-us, Emmanuel, meant God in Auschwitz.

2. The notion of pro-existence has been developed to express the whole dynamism which resides in the *pro nobis*. Jesus died for us, and that also means that he died in our favour, for our benefit. A rapid analysis of the *hyper* formulas contained in the New Testament shows that the existential attitude of Jesus has strongly influenced the post-Easter community. The attitude of Jesus, the man for others, sums up in his death the whole power of the life that he receives. The last supper of Jesus with his disciples is the topic of pro-existence. This basic attitude of Jesus corresponds to that of God, who does not exist for himself but always in movement towards the other. Being for others constitutes the profound essence of Jesus.[25] Those who are marked by the collective dramas of the twentieth century are in search of this Christ for others and discover in Jesus that he was orientated on others and on the Wholly Other.[26] Jesus stripped himself of his divinity, and that is his greatness. Xavier Tilliette is right in emphasizing that the theology of kenosis to which we are sensitive today is full of affectivity.[27] The experience of death cannot be turned completely into a theory. Now the idea of pro-existence integrates this notion of kenosis by the very fact that death is perceived as the human experience which gives the incarnation of God in Jesus Christ its definitive character. For some writers, that means that after the Holocaust, the cross expresses the full sense of the incarnation.[28] To escape from the aporias that the shock of the Holocaust has produced, christological soteriology has every interest in giving to the pro-existence of Jesus, in solidarity with human suffering, the central character that it deserves. A theology of pro-existence presupposes that one engages in strict, serious and demanding reflection on otherness, as, for example, does E. Levinas. Jesus, the man for others, is the opposite of the negation of the other. In obeying (listening to) the Father, Jesus is the *sym-pathetic, com-passionate* God.

3. But is there room for hope in the face of horror? The cry of Jesus on the cross did not end up in the void. Beyond the experience of being dead and remaining dead among the dead, God raises Jesus in response to his yes to Sheol. Human beings, defined by the Greeks as *pantos poros*, those who find openings and ways for all situations, are *aporos* in the face of death. Only Christ opens up ways. The cry of Jesus on the cross is the cry of all humanity to God. Christian hope is at the foot of the cross. It seeks to see in the cry of the crucified Jesus the cry of hope which sets everything on God. Certainly, a large number of Jews and Christians in Auschwitz and in the

gulags died in this hope. We only have to think of Maximilian Kolbe. L. Caza remarks that paradoxically the cry of Jesus on the cross meets up with the groaning of creation evoked in Romans 8.[29] Such classic soteriological themes as those of substitution or representation become much more topical in face of the horrors which mark this century. In presenting Jesus for the condemnation of the crowd, Pilate presents the man. *Ecce homo*, here is the man Jesus, here too is the fragile humanity which God comes to join. The Creator is involved in this presentation of Jesus to the crowd, since human beings are in the image and likeness of God. As for the Spirit, it makes memory of this moment in which God is outraged, so as not to lose hope in the little ones and the oppressed. 'You will be as gods,' promised the tempter to Adam and Eve, and that is the fantasy of the ideologists of the twentieth century. 'Behold the man': God unites himself with what happens, fragile and bruised. Only in this passage is there the strange word of the cross and does there dwell the promise made to all the damned of the earth, 'today you will be with me'.

Translated by John Bowden

Notes

1. M. Knutsen, 'The Holocaust in Theology and Philosophy: The Question of Truth', *Concilium* 175, 1984, 74.
2. H. Schuermann, *Comment Jesus a-t-il vécu sa mort?*, Paris 1977, 181.
3. Karl Barth, *Church Dogmatics* II.2, Edinburgh 1957, 177.
4. Justin, *Dialogue with Trypho*, 131.2. See the excellent study by M. Gourgues, *Le crucifié, du scandale à l'exaltation*, Paris 1988, 74–87.
5. E. Jüngel, *God as the Mystery of the World*, Edinburgh and Grand Rapids 1983, I, 218.
6. P. J. Labarrière, *Le Christ avenir*, Paris 1983, 146.
7. Ibid., 29.
8. F. Varillon, *La souffrance de Dieu*, Paris 1975, 60.
9. H. Urs von Balthasar, *Theodramatik* IV, *Das Endspiel*, Einsiedeln 1983, 191–222.
10. *Letter to Polycarp*, II.2.
11. *On the Pasch*, III.
12. E. Jüngel, *God as the Mystery of the World* (n. 5), 219.
13. Origen, *Homily on Ezekiel*, VI.6.
14. Thomas Aquinas, *Summa Theologica* Ia q.21, a.3.
15. J. P. Jossua, *Le Dieu de la foi chrétienne*, Paris 1989, 88.
16. W. Kasper, *The God of Jesus Christ*, London and New York 1984, 162.
17. O. Hofius (ed.), *Reflexionen finsterer Zeit. Zwei Vorträge von Fritz Stern und Hans Jonas*, Tübingen 1948; H. Jonas, *Der Gottesbegriff nach Auschwitz. Eine*

jüdische Stimme, Baden-Baden 1987.

18. Jonas, *Gottesbegriff* (n. 16), 24–6.

19. Ibid., 42.

20. Ibid., 47.

21. S. Shapiro, 'Hearing the Testimony of Radical Negation', *Concilium* 175, 1984, 10 nn.18,19.

22. W. Maas, 'Jusq'où est descendu le Fils?', *Communio* VI.1, *Descendu aux enfers*, Paris 1981, 11.

23. H. Urs von Balthasar, *Le mystère pascal*, Paris 1972, 47.

24. J. M. Lustiger, 'Ce vide des lieux et du temps ne peut qu'être regardé que loin, avec foi', in *Supplément de La Documentation Catholique 1991* (1 January 1989), 29.

25. W. Kasper, *Jesus the Christ*, London 1976, 167f.

26. Schuermann, *Comment Jesus a-t-il vécu sa mort?* (n. 2), 166.

27. X. Tilliette, 'L'exinanition du Christ: théologie de la kénose', in *Les quatre fleuves*, IV, 1975, 48.

28. J. Pawlikowski, 'The Holocaust and Contemporary Christology', *Concilium* 175, 1984, 46.

29. L. Caza, *'Mon dieu, pourquoi m'as tu abandonné?' comme Bonne Nouvelle de Jésus Christ, Fils de Dieu, comme Bonne Nouvelle de Dieu pour la multitude*, Montreal and Paris 1989, 516.

The Language of Remembrance: Reflections on the Theological Discussion of the Phenomenon of Mass Death

Werner Jeanrond

In an age of almost perfect world-wide communication, news about accidents, natural catastrophes, wars and epidemics has become a fixed ingredient of daily media fare. Every day the phenomenon of mass death happens somewhere in the world, and every day it again proves too much for our emotion, mind, spirit and language to cope with. While it is possible to draw up statistics of hundreds, thousands and millions of victims, compare them and evaluate them, these statistics do not allow us any direct personal contact with the victims. We can lament mass death, research its causes and background, investigate who is directly to blame and who has a share in the blame, i.e. treat mass death as a 'case' like any other event in our world, but can we really understand the full scope of mass death? Do we have any form of language in which we can get nearer to the phenomenon of mass death? Are there means of theological expression which could make it possible to think of the simultaneous death of many people in a way which is at all appropriate? Or are very narrow limits set to our capacity for thought and remembrance in this respect?

In this article I want to attempt to discuss answers to these questions. First of all I shall go briefly into the difficulties in dealing with the phenomenon of death generally which are characteristic of our time. Then I hope to show that the remembrance of the dead is a necessary element of Christian believing. Finally I shall attempt to sound out the possibilities and limits of Christian discussion of the phenomenon of mass death.

I. Contemporary difficulties in dealing with death

Dying and death provoke very different reactions in the Western industrial nations: either both phenomena of human existence are ignored and shifted into the purely private sphere, or they are staged publicly as a breathtaking spectacle. The usual death of an individual is normally communicated to a wider public only by a paid-for announcement in the paper, whereas the spectacular death of a so-called media personality can command our attention over a longer period.

For example, the death of individuals in the course of what has now become an intensified practice of execution in the United States is celebrated as a public event and transmitted to all television viewers at home. 'The countdown of the last days and hours is followed by colossal media coverage, transmitted by a large number of television stations with live reports about the place of execution, the demonstrations and counter-demonstrations that go with it, discussions with experts, interviews with members of the families of both parties who have travelled there, with politicians, pastors and the public, links to the state and federal authorities concerned with the case and so on.'[1] Plane crashes are now packaged for the media in a similar way and commentaries are given on wars. On the one hand this exploits the human drama of struggle with premature death, and on the other it leaves it to television viewers whether or not they take part in events of this kind, by switching on or off. So the reality of death expressed in this way cannot ultimately claim to be able to challenge viewers to serious reaction, especially as they have long been blunted to what they see by the many fictitious deaths in crime films on the screen. Death on the television suffers from an increasing loss of reality, despite and because of its frequency and colossal presentation. So there is a danger that precisely because of the way in which they treat death, the media make what is already a strange event even stranger to us.

As there is no serious discussion about dealing with death among the public generally, the question arises how there can be any Christian reflection on death and on mass death in such a context. There is also the question whether Christianity itself is not to some degree also responsible for this trivial treatment of death today, in that it has tacitly or quite officially tolerated or encouraged the blurring of the boundary between death and immortality.

If human death seems only to be a not very pretty passage of the soul, separated from the body, to one or another form of 'eternal life', and no longer a radical question about the meaning of life and the creative presence of God, important horizons for the human understanding of death are lost. It is birth and death which first give human beings their time. If death is now rationalized away, human existence must appear timeless and thus an infinite continuum without any serious interruption. With its traditional doctrine of the detailed course of the journey of the soul to death, supported with images like purgatory, heaven, hell, indulgences and so on, the Roman Catholic Church and Roman Catholic theology in particular have contributed to the rationalizing of the human understanding of death and time. In this way death is prevented from posing a radical question. The creative power of death which is hidden in the question it raises is then skimmed off by the institutional church, which feels itself responsible for the safe passage of the soul through death. In such a way the radical question of the meaning of life which emerges from death can be administratively undermined or institutionally automated.

On the other hand, however, the eschatological experiences contained in these traditional images must not be argued away; otherwise our reference to hope in God's future is degraded so that it becomes a simple concept. 'Consequently what we have to say about the consummation, if it is not to be either too sensuously abstruse or too anaemic and abstract, must move on the borderline between image and concept. At the same time experience is indispensable as a correlative if the metaphors are not to evaporate into abstractions; but experience is by no means the sole criterion if our images are not to degenerate into wish-images.'[2]

For the church which deals with death in the way indicated above, the experience of mass death is more of a quantitative problem: for how many people has the dividing line between time and eternity become reality? So thinking of a great many dead at the same time is just a matter of organization for a church whose pastoral approach has been automated, and is not necessarily already a challenge to our concept of God and our traditional relationship to God and the world. But it is precisely these definitions of the relationship that have become problematical for some Jewish and Christian thinkers in the face of the experiences of mass death in our century.

II. Remembrance as part of our believing

The experience of the mass death of millions of Jews in the concentration camps of Nazi Germany has been described by numerous Jewish and Christian thinkers as a caesura in thought and feeling. In his book *The Tremendum: A Theological Interpretation of the Holocaust*, published in

1981, the Jewish scholar Arthur A. Cohen wrote that he could not speak about Auschwitz for almost a generation, 'for I had no language that tolerated the immensity of the wound'.[3] But instead of surrendering to speechlessness and thus to the obliteration of the memory of the monstrous crime, Cohen was concerned to develop a way of thinking which despite all dangers and weaknesses approaches in language the phenomenon of violent mass death. Borrowing the term from Rudolf Otto, Cohen speaks of the Holocaust as a *tremendum*. 'I call the death camps the *tremendum*, for it is the monument of a meaningless inversion of life to an orgiastic celebration of death, to a psychosexual and pathological degeneracy unparalleled and unfathomable to any person bonded to life.'[4] So can we make any intellectual approach at all to this phenomenon? Cohen answers this question as follows: 'The judgment that thought is inadequate to the *tremendum* is, in one sense, based upon a logical fallacy, for it is never suggested that thought can number six million particularities, or, for that matter, the hundred million slain in this century's wars of skill and ideology. The fact that the mind cannot contain such particularity is not a mark of the incommensurability of thought, but only of memory's inability to particularize each loss.'[5]

Cohen calls for the *tremendum* to be treated as a historical and a theological reality, which insists on a new reading of Jewish meaning.[6] So the *tremendum* is at the same time a caesura and a new beginning.[7] Like numerous Christian theologians Cohen, too, sees this break as being so significant because it puts the traditional concept of God radically in question. 'I cannot address myself to the implication that the *tremendum* has for Christian theology, although I cannot believe that any Christian theology of a God *who has already saved* can make much sense after the *tremendum*.'[8] So the experience of the *tremendum* calls for a new beginning in talking of God and a new reflection on human freedom and its need for reconciliation. 'The *tremendum* remains *tremendum*, neither diminished nor explained, but nonetheless limned by interpretation.'[9]

Cohen's effort to tackle the historical and theological significance of the Holocaust for our present-day thought is a warning to us not to be silent in the face of the experience of this violent mass death. Our thought remains obligated to memory, even if it can never do justice to the phenomenon with which it struggles. The alternative to this fragmentary concern with Jewish mass death would be silence, and that would be to exterminate the victims once again, now from our memory. So Cohen argues against all those who think that the only appropriate answer to organized mass death is silence.

Johann Baptist Metz similarly pleads for remembrance, thought and reflection after Auschwitz. 'In the face of Auschwitz there can be no abstention, no dissociation; where that is attempted it would again be secret complicity with a horror which has not been understood.'[10] Like Cohen, Metz interprets the Holocaust as a caesura: 'We Christians can never go back behind Auschwitz; to be precise we can no longer get beyond Auschwitz by ourselves, but only together with the victims.'[11] The basic categories of theological thought which Metz has developed in his *magnum opus Glaube in Geschichte und Gesellschaft*, namely remembrance, narrative and solidarity, allow theological thought to enter into the victims of violent mass death, though of course none of these categories can fully comprehend the horror of the Holocaust. For Metz, remembrance has 'a central meaning with a theological foundation in its form as "solidarity backwards", as solidarity of memory with the dead and defeated which breaks the spell of history as the history of the victors – whether interpreted in evolutionary or dialectical terms'.[12] Remembrance is a multi-dimensional event. It relates to the memory of suffering and the rescue of identity, and it offers resistance to, interrupts, the course of things and ideas, making the use of human freedom in the historical process a problem to be dealt with. So it necessarily has a narrative structure.[13]

Metz repeatedly stresses the basic narrative version of Christian faith, though of course he does not want to dispense with argumentative reason. Rather, he is concerned to criticize a theology which consists purely in argument. 'In the face of the history of human suffering a purely argumentative theology which does not constantly make its origin present again in narrative remembrance leads to those thousand modifications in its argument under which imperceptibly any identifiable content of Christian faith evaporates.'[14]

Both Cohen and Metz show us impressively that the experience of violent mass death in our century must not condemn either the Jewish or the Christian intellectual tradition to silence. Rather, both traditions are called on to understand the experience of violent mass death as a caesura of thought and to take it seriously as a challenge to new thought for a new praxis of belief in God. So in both traditions the necessarily fragmentary discussion of the *tremendum* has also led to a methodological reflection on the basic anamnetic categories of belief in God. Here it was not a matter of a linear narration of the relationship between human beings and God but of a relationship which is constantly interrupted and disturbed by suffering and death.

III. Possibilities and limits of the Christian discussion of the phenomenon of mass death

In the previous section we were concerned with mass death resulting from human violence, but not yet with mass death which affects people as the result of unplanned disasters, like plane crashes, earthquakes, epidemics and floods. Despite the important differences in the cause of the two phenomena, which must not be trivialized or levelled down, they do have some things in common. Too many demands are put on our understanding and our particular capacity for remembrance by the experience even of mass death which is caused by accidents. The simultaneous and unmerited death of many people in an accident also raises questions for our understanding of God, though these relate less to the theoretical understanding of human freedom than to the understanding of the nature of God's creation. Why must people die a premature death? Why must we live in a universe in which there is incomprehensible suffering which is no one's fault?

Any experience of human suffering and above all of any premature human death[15] raises radical questions about the meaning of our existence. In our search for answers to such questions we also keep coming across the efforts of earlier generations of people to cope with the phenomenon of premature death. For example, the Jewish wisdom literature is emphatically concerned with the fate of the innocent victim, both the individual and the people as a whole. Although the scriptures of Israel do not discuss the phenomenon of mass death caused by violence or disaster which is familiar to us today, they do speak of the human struggle with misfortune. Here death as a normal phenomenon of human temporality does not seem to be the real problem (cf. Sirach 41). But the premature death of the innocent brings unexpected and serious suffering and therefore raises the question of the nature of the divine counsels.

So while Job struggles with a fate which he cannot understand, he persistently refuses to follow his friends in accepting a dualism between good and evil powers in the world which would explain his fate. Instead of this he recognizes the mystery of the divine counsels and holds fast to God's will, believing it to be good even if he cannot understand it. Job's suffering remains as an unexplained appeal to God's wisdom.[16]

The cry of the innocent victim also keeps appearing in the Psalms. In Psalm 10 we hear the cry of the persecuted innocent: 'Arise, O God, lift up your hand! Do not forget the afflicted!' (v. 16). However, this cry of suffering finally ends up, like that of Job, in a confession of the lordship of

God (v. 16). The assertion of the innocence of the people oppressed by war in Ps. 44 and the call for God's help in this tribulation represent an interruption in the usual confidence of salvation. So the Hebrew scriptures do not only offer a salvation-historical reading of the relationship with God but at the same time also a question about the meaning of suffering and unmerited premature death which continually interrupts this confidence.

Neither the problem of evil and the associated phenomenon of mass death caused by violence nor the problem of unmerited disaster and the associated phenomenon of mass death can be overcome at the level of theoretical thought. In a much-noted article, Paul Ricoeur has referred to the first part of this double problem, the impossibility of overcoming the problem of evil purely theoretically; his thoughts also seem to me to fit the second part of the problem, mass death caused by disasters.[17] In this article Ricoeur stresses that insight into the failure of theoretical approaches in the face of evil must not lead to passiveness. Rather, 'action and the catharsis of feelings are called upon not to give a solution but a response, a response able to render the aporia productive'.[18] Ricoeur distinguishes three stages in such an answer. First, it is important to integrate into our mourning insight into our ignorance in this respect. Secondly, Ricoeur recommends that one should be allowed to express lament over a disaster as an accusation against God: 'Our accusation against God is here the impatience of hope. It has its origin in the cry of the psalmist, "How long, O Lord?"'[19] 'A third stage in the catharsis of the lament is to discover that the reasons for believing in God have nothing in common with the need to explain the origin of suffering . . . To believe in God *in spite of* . . . is one of the ways in which we can integrate the speculative aporia into the work of mourning.'[20]

So the experience of mass death does not condemn us either to complete speechlessness or to passivity, despite our inability to understand this phenomenon theoretically. We can express our mourning in words; we can articulate in words our grief over our intellectual inability to cope with premature human death; and we can formulate our protest to God. In short, we can mourn in words. Numerous writers offer us support in this process.[21] Moreover as Christians we can also give expression to our hope that our creator God, who has committed himself to silence for the sake of our freedom, suffers with us in this very silence, and in this way makes his solidarity known to us as he made it known to his Son Jesus Christ, delivered over to the hopelessness of death on the cross. So the recollection of the suffering of countless people can be taken up into remembrance of the suffering of Jesus Christ. Jesus' cry on the cross and our cry in the face of the victims of violent death, or death caused by disasters, can become the beginning of a new hope. The lamentation over suffering interrupts any theological system of thought and in this way makes room for new speech, new thought, new action. Remembrance of the suffering of Jesus and the solidarity of God as this was experienced in a surprising way by the friends of Jesus after his death open up to us on the one hand the possibility of remembering all the nameless disaster and misfortune of our time and on the other the hope that God will turn his face equally to the victims of all this suffering.

So the terrible experience of mass death more than ever calls our faith out of its passivity to active engagement against all premature death which is organized by us human beings and for which we are to blame. This battle of believers against death is not against death as the natural limit of human life which is imposed on us by God's creation, but against all forms of death which are caused for us by human beings themselves. However, beyond this the question why innocent people keep dying premature deaths as a result of misfortunes remains unanswered. We do not know why we have to live in a universe which is not stable but constantly keeps changing, in which children die of cancer and countless people are exterminated by earthquakes. All our speculations are doomed to failure. So all that remains is the cry to God, remembrance of the victims and hope of God's salvation.

Translated by John Bowden

Notes

1. Edmund Arens, 'Baseball, Basketball and Hinrichtungen: USA: Vollstreckung der Todesstrafe als Medienereignis', *Orientierung* 56, 1992, 196.

2. Hans Küng, *Eternal Life*, London and New York 1984, reissued 1991, 220.

3. Arthur A. Cohen, *The Tremendum: A Theological Interpretation of the Holocaust*, New York 1981, 37.

4. Ibid., 19.

5. Ibid., 41.

6. Ibid., 51f.

7. Ibid., 58.

8. Ibid., 76–7.

9. Ibid., 95.

10. Johann Baptist Metz, *Jenseits bürgerlicher Religion: Reden über die Zukunft des Christentums*, Munich and Mainz 1980, 31.

11. Ibid., 47.

12. Johann Baptist Metz, *Glaube in Geschichte und Gesellschaft: Studien zu einer praktischen Fundamentaltheologie*, Mainz 1977, 161.

13. See also Johann Baptist Metz, 'Für eine anamnetische Kultur', *Orientierung* 56, 1992, 205–7.

14. Ibid., 190.

15. By premature death I understand dying before the end of what could be expected biologically to be a normal life span. I am well aware of the difficulties of arriving at a definition of the biological life span. But here it must be firmly maintained that there is such a thing as 'too early' a death, which raises different questions from the 'normal' end of a human life. See Eberhard Jüngel, *Tod*, Stuttgart 1971, 170f.

16. See also Gerhard von Rad, *Wisdom in Israel*, London 1972, 224–6.

17. Paul Ricoeur, 'Evil. A Challenge to Philosophy and Theology', in *Journal of the American Academy of Religion*, 53, 1985, 635–48.

18. Ibid., 644.

19. Ibid., 647.

20. Ibid.

21. Cf. also the poems 'Todesfuge' by Paul Celan, 'In den Silos der Qual' by Horst Bienek, and 'Beschwörung' by Marie Luise Kaschnitz, in Horst Bingel (ed.), *Deutsche Lyrik: Gedichte seit 1945*, Stuttgart 1961, and the essays by George Steiner in his book *Language and Silence: Essays 1958–1966*, London and Boston 1985.

III · Keeping Memory

When Remembering Brings Redemption: Faith and the Armenian Genocide

Vigen Guroian

Like Narekatsi the visionary of centuries past
I send this supplication to You, my creator.
I the sinful poet of a dying century
with feverish blood infested with the live bacteria
waited for the anxiously expected dawn
and saw it change into a blood sunset,
while the faithful stood by red-eyed,
with light in their eyes. Now the sun returns
from the West in the name of holy bread
but rises like a lifted medieval axe.

Eghishe Charents, *Prayer to God from the Depths of My Heart* (1936)

Something devastating happened to Armenian Christianity as a result of genocide. For some Armenians faith became impossible. For many the habit persisted but not the conviction. For yet others faith was for ever changed by the evident incapacity or unwillingness of God to intervene and stop the slaughter of innocents. Sadly, no contemporary Armenian theology has answered the agonized cry of the Armenian poets. No Armenian theology yet has emerged which provides strong resources to translate the sad and sometimes bitter remembering into a redemptive experience. In a response to *Concilium*'s request that I write about 'how the Armenian people express their tragic remembrance of genocide', the voices of Armenian poets such as Eghishe Charents remain a haunting reminder of the tragedy that the genocide has been for faith. Thus, in an ever so modest fashion, I will endeavour here briefly not only to describe how the genocide has been reflected in faith but also to mark off the general lines of the unfinished task of appropriate theological and pastoral response to the lingering wounds of victimization among Armenians.

Complex reactions

In recent years, Donald E. Miller and Lorna Touryan Miller have studied through the use of oral history techniques some of the traumatic as well as transforming religious effects of the Armenian genocide upon survivors. The Millers have documented patterns of denial, rationalization, resignation, reconciliation, rage and revenge in the lives of survivors and their children. For example, anger at God, sometimes leading to a complete denial of God, is a well-known phenomenon among survivors of the Armenocide and their children. 'How could God have allowed this to happen, especially to a people who were the first to adopt Christianity as a state religion?' And there is the always present voice which raises the disturbing rumination, 'Armenians wonder if God is on their side. I think they feel life happens to them, and they are powerless in life to do anything about their lot.' Alluding to the story of how God gave Armenians left-over rocks for their land, the Armenian woman whom I have just quoted mused in an interview with the *Hartford Courant*, part of a feature article prompted by the earthquake disaster of December 1988: 'Armenians choose their destiny. The destiny they choose is rocks, because they don't know there's land out there.'' Even in this secular time, God and self are very much the poles of Armenian identity. On the surface, this woman's comments appear quite contradictory. On the one hand, Armenians have been powerless, subject to the whim of an inscrutable God. On the other hand, Armenians chose their own destiny and God obliged. Who is in control, God or humanity? An impossible mix of hatred of God and of self-hatred colours post-genocide Armenian consciousness.

Other Armenians, the Millers note, continue as best they can to hold on to more traditional conceptions of God and his relationship to the Armenian people. One individual the Millers interviewed said: 'God used the Turks as a club for us. We had the light but did not give it to the Turks. As a Christian nation we lived as atheists.' Frequently the comment was made, 'It's not understandable on human terms. God's ways are not our ways. It's all a very great mystery now, but in heaven we will find the answers to our many whys.' The Millers conclude: 'Hence, religious justification would seem to emerge from a world-view that says God is in control of the universe and therefore there must be some meaning to the Armenian genocide.'[2]

At the source of this reaction to the genocide has been an unrelieved sense of affliction – an Armenian woundedness and experience of being powerless to do anything about the pain of unjustly inflicted suffering. The pathologies in Armenian life traceable to this unanswered suffering among the survivors of the genocide and succeeding generations are well known to those who have studied the psychology of post-genocide Armenian life. One of the most disturbing symptoms of this pathology in the national life was the outbreak of Armenian terrorism in the 1970s–80s. As I write, Armenians carrying the memory of genocide resist and fight Azeris on the borders of Armenia and in Nagorno-Karabagh. Armenians view the Azeris as Turkic enemies bent upon the destruction of the Armenian people. Among such a persecuted people collective 'paranoia' is triggered by real and unreal threats to national existence.

On a world-wide scale one easily observes in Armenians other persisting symptoms of the pathology of the victim. There is that all too well known phenomenon among diaspora Armenians of keeping count of Armenians who have 'made it' among the non-Armenians (i.e. among those who really have power over their lives). Just beneath the Armenian boastfulness about being the first Christian nation are deep psychological wounds and insecurities. Much of this pain and insecurity of Armenian existence was brought about by the sheer immensity of the genocide in the numbers and percentages of the total population lost. Between 1915–1922 the total population of Armenians living within Turkey – especially in the historic Armenian provinces of eastern Turkey – was reduced from two million to no more than several hundred thousand. Somewhere between one million and one and one half million Armenians had lost their lives in forced marches of deportation and blood massacres. Ancient centres of Armenian culture and learning were wiped clean of Armenians and historic monuments were deliberately destroyed or left in ruins. Nearly all Armenian communities in the diaspora carry the memory of the genocide through survivors and their progeny. One must add to this the continuing history of Turkish denial and the betrayal of nations from whom Armenians expected sympathy and acknowledgment of the crimes committed against them.

Suffering and the dead ends of denial and rationalization

Intense suffering is sometimes a hindrance to faith. When that suffering has been brought about by a great injustice and others are unwilling to recognize it, this adds difficulty for dealing with the pain of suffering. These things are, perhaps, the sources of the massive denial and repression of suffering in Armenian theology and Armenian life generally since the Armenocide. If we look carefully at the Millers' examples of response to the genocide experience and the testimony of the woman interviewed in the *Hartford Courant* article, we happen upon some of the well travelled routes by which Armenians have reached the dead ends of denied and repressed suffering. One dead end is to blame God. The anger and self-hatred for belonging to a murdered people is transferred to God. But God then becomes an ever-present reminder of an unanswered humiliation and psychological pain. Another dead end is to blame the Armenian people. God is excused. But at the cost of self-hatred. Self-forgiveness becomes impossible. Of course, the Turk is blamed. But when he does not accept the blame, the anger and pain have no place to go but 'underground', into the depths of one's own psyche. Self-hatred, the nagging sense of inferiority or feelings of victimization become the almost inevitable accompaniments of post-genocide Armenian identity.

Massive rationalizations which derive substance from a romanticized memory of past national glory and fantastic projections of future national success figure prominently in the collective and personal repression of suffering within the post-genocide Armenian psyche. I cannot tell the whole of this story here. But suffice it to say that sadly the Armenian church also has contributed to these processes of repression and rationalization. Resurrection is the most used and abused of the religious symbols which the church has invoked in its own misconceived ministry to the nation. God promises resurrection of the Armenian nation. God promises Armenian empowerment as a compensation for injustices against the Armenian people. God promises that the Armenian people will receive justice. God has been victorious in the resurrection and promises the same to the Armenian people.

This rhetoric has rent resurrection from the whole cloth of the gospel account of Christ's passion, death and resurrection. Why has the Armenian church misrepresented, even if at times unwittingly, the gospel account of suffering and redemption? The main reason, I believe, is that the church has wanted to play the role of the leader of both the spiritual people of God and the secular nation. It has insisted, in the face of modern reality and the gospel story of a Saviour crucified by the world, that the church and the nation are one. It has perpetuated the myth that Armenia still is a Christian nation. The Armenian church has sought to be the bearer of a hope on terms acceptable to all Armenians, believers and non-believers alike. In order to be something to everyone it has suppressed the gospel of a crucified God and Christian discipleship in the way of the cross. It has wanted to claim all Armenians as members of the body of Christ in the face of its own deep knowledge rooted in the scriptures that not all people have faith or will have faith even to the end of this age. It has been the victim of its own deep denial.

If these are some of the wrong paths of remembering which Armenians have followed and even the church has fostered, what might be a right, truthful and redemptive way of remembering? How might faith in Jesus Christ as Lord and Saviour grip the hearts and minds of Armenians so that individuals and community are healed and given hope? Some fifteen years ago, I began collecting oral histories of survivors of the Armenian genocide. Among those whose stories I recorded were members of the Richmond, Virginia, Armenian community, where my wife June was raised and we lived at the time. One of these was a lady, born in Zeitun in south central Turkey. When she was a small child her family moved to nearby Marash where in the spring of 1915 the deportations began. Her father had already been conscripted into the Turkish military, never again to be seen by his family, presumably a victim of the Turkish policy of conscripting Armenian males into the military and executing them. She and her remaining family were marched that year across Turkey into the Syrian desert, a march which in her memory lasted for ever. During the journey, this young girl of seven witnessed the deaths of some seventy relatives. Only she and her mother survived.

At the close of our final meeting together, I asked her how she could believe in God in view of her great personal loss and tragedy. At first she demurred. She said that she was not a priest or a theologian. I insisted, surely she had thought about this matter. 'Yes,' she said, she had. Some of the men and women of her generation had succumbed to bitterness and resentment, even anger against God. They would accuse God, 'Why did God do this to us?' She, however, had not grown bitter. There were, of course, moments of doubt and questioning even at this time in her life. But her memories would return to her grandfather, a man of exceptional faith. For often during those terrible, violent days of the march, when she was tired and her small feet ached and she was thirsty and hungry and wanted to stop but did not for fear of the soldiers' whip, she would ask her grandfather: '"Grandpa, where are we going?" He would answer, "We are going to Jerusalem." I began to hate Jerusalem. I would say, "I don't

like Jerusalem. I want to go home," and there would be tears in his eyes. He
was weeping. But I did not know why. Only now I understand.'

This patriarch of her family died in Syria. However, before his death he
left his family with a command and a final request. He said: 'Even if they
should put a knife to your neck, do not deny your faith. Death lasts only
one moment. Renouncing your faith means giving up an eternity of joy
with God.' And he requested that he be given a Christian burial. And he
was. Whereas the little girl saw others who had died carried away by oxen
cart to unmarked mass graves, her grandfather was buried by his
daughter-in-law. He had asked that at his burial a passage from II Timothy
be read. She could not recall the identity of the passage. But I do not doubt
that it was II Timothy 4.6–8. 'As for me, already my life is being poured
out on the altar, and the hour for my departure is upon me. I have run the
great race, I have finished the course, I have kept faith. And now the prize
awaits me, the great garland (crown) of righteousness, which the Lord, the
all-just judge, will award me on that great Day; and it is not for me alone,
but for all who have set their hearts on his coming appearance.' The lady
finished by saying, 'As I remember my grandfather, I also remember Jesus
when he was crucified. This is what gives me hope and sustains me. And I
believe in the resurrection and that we will live even after this death on
Earth . . . Maybe God means the Armenians to be an example for the
world.'

The answer to how the Armenian memory of the Armenocide might
become a redemptive remembering was answered for me more than fifteen
years ago in these words spoken by a survivor of the genocide. Every April
24th, Armenians in all places mark a day of remembrance for those who
died as victims and as martyrs of the Armenian genocide. On that day, year
after year, the Armenian church has joined in the demand for justice. Yet
even those outsiders most sympathetic to the Armenian cause have advised
Armenians that while justice is important there is no guarantee it will
come; nor may it be what is most needed. The emphasis should be on truth
and healing even more than justice. 'Maybe,' the lady said, 'God means for
Armenians to be an example to the Earth.' How might this be so? The
immediate concern of Armenians after the Ottoman Turk struck his awful
blow at them was to find a way to survive, to nurture the orphaned nation in
all the strange new lands into which its members had been exiled. Then in
1965 with the commemoration of the fiftieth anniversary of the genocide, a
new consciousness began to emerge. Armenians found the will and the way
to voice the anger, the outrage and the pain of what had happened to them,
to their parents and grandparents. This served its purpose. In its best light

this activity raised the consciousness of Armenians to the significance of the genocide for them and for other people. It was the first genocide of this century, the awful predecessor of the Holocaust and all the human slaughter and state inflicted mass murder which is the mark of this century. These lessons served as the foundation upon which the seventieth and seventy-fifth commemorations were built. Remembering the genocide spurred Armenians to wage the argument for restoration of the Armenian historic land and an independent nation. It has been the occasion for pressuring Turkey to admit finally that indeed a genocide was perpetrated and Ottoman Turkey was responsible. Remembering one's own tragedy has meant adding a voice to the universal plea for human rights and the prevention of genocide. But beyond even these causes is the necessary condition that Armenians witness to the faith which makes the martyrs of the genocide alive with God.

Faith and remembering

There is a story told by the Armenian writer Teotig who collected accounts of the clergy and their martyrdom during the Great Catastrophe. One day in 1915, as in so many Armenian towns and villages, the 800 families of Kourd Belen (Turkish, meaning Wolf's Hill) near Izmit, the ancient Nicomedia, were given orders to abandon their homes and form a caravan of deportation. The pastor of the village was an eighty-five year old priest, Fr Khoren Hambartzoumian, who for all his years as a priest had served the people of Kourd Belen. Fr Hambartzoumian was instructed to lead his people out from the village. As the procession of bewildered and frightened Armenians reached the outskirts of the village, neighbouring Turks came out to view the exiles, and taunted the priest, calling to him, 'Good luck, old man. Whom are you going to bury today?' The old man replied: 'Yes, God is dead and we are rushing to his funeral.'

Who is to say for sure what lay in the heart of Fr Khoren Hambartzoumian as he uttered the words 'Yes, God is dead and we are rushing to his funeral'? Beyond the moral and political significance of the Armenian genocide, there is a profound religious dimension. A Jewish theologian of the Holocaust has written: 'God suffers not on account of what man does to him. What could man do to God? He suffers because of what man does to himself and his brother. He suffers the suffering of his servant, the agony of the guiltless. In all their affliction, he is afflicted.'[3] I have said already that Armenians who would follow Christ need to learn that the issue is not one of justice alone. Rather, this tragic event challenges

Armenians to think about how those who confess that Jesus Christ is Lord can make of the suffering and dying of the one and one half million a righteous witness to his promise of eternal life. I know that the lady whose story I have told meant just this when she contemplated the greater purpose to which God intended Armenians to put their suffering.

One would have hoped that Armenians, having endured the death of their physical body, the loss of the earthly homeland, and been dispersed throughout the world as sojourners in strange lands, could have recaptured their biblical minds, for Armenians are a biblical people. Thus far they have not. Questing for human justice, they have been distracted from their godly calling. The genocide memory needs to be recalled in tandem with the biblical vision which shaped Armenians as a people. Armenians might then rededicate themselves to that Christian witness and discipleship which their forebears so willingly took up and for which so many of them gave up their lives.

Suffering and Christian discipleship: the way to healing and hope

The Bible does show a way out of suffering into hope. In the Christian scriptures that hope is in Jesus Christ who suffered and died on the cross for the sins of all and promised eternal life to those who would *believe* in him and *follow* him even to a cross. If we are truly followers and imitators of Jesus Christ, then, as the grandfather said to the little girl, we are all sojourners on our way to Jerusalem. The Lord of resurrection and life invites human beings freely to follow him, but the path they must take once they have decided to do so is one already trodden by him up the rock of Golgotha with the awful weight of the cross upon his back and the agony of the crucifixion before him. For Christ, the glory of Palm Sunday was followed by the humiliation of that Friday which those who follow him dare call Good because in faith they have the hope for life eternal, since he has trampled Death down for us by death. Is it, therefore, so incomprehensible that the glory of Christian Armenia should in time have been revealed as the prelude to the Golgotha of 1915? Armenians had more than intimations of this throughout their history: the early persecutions under foreign domination, the devastation of the Memeluke invaders, the slave yoke of Ottoman rule.

Suffering and its memory need to be placed in the context of Christian discipleship. Christ did not seek the crucifixion. Suffering is not something God wants us to seek either. Suffering is not a necessity of the

Christian life. But if one follows Christ faithfully in an unrighteous world, suffering is inevitable. 'If the world hates you, be aware that it hated me before it hated you. If you belonged to the world, the world would love you as its own; because you do not belong to the world – therefore the world hates you' (John 15.18–19). The full meaning of resurrection is only understood in this light. It is God's earnest that paradoxically the Son's death on the tree was also a victory over death for all who believe in him.

Thus, Christians remember the cross and the resurrection in eucharistic liturgy because they wish to thank God for the victory over suffering and death he has made possible for them in Jesus Christ. But God also expects our gratitude to be accompanied by a witness to the truth of salvation through service to others who are suffering and our intercession in prayer on their behalf. Several years ago, on one memorable evening in Armenia when the electricity had gone off, I sat in darkness pierced by the light of a single candle with a grief-stricken father who had lost his son in the earthquake of December 1989. He told me of three dreadful days during which he searched for his children and located them buried beneath ten stories of rubble in their apartment house, and how his young son and daughter were dug out. Lillet survived but Armen, who had given his sister the courage to hope, died of internal injuries. Kevork said he had been arguing with God; but that God would not answer for himself. 'I will go on living my life as I must,' he pleaded, 'but I can no longer be concerned with what God's purposes might be.' 'Kevork,' I responded, 'surely you know that this will not be enough.' He answered, 'What else is left for me?' Kevork and I read the Bible together that night. We turned to the final chapter of the Book of Job. We read aloud together how God scolded Job's friends for not having 'spoken of me what is right, as my servant Job has'. And God told them: '"[M]y servant Job shall pray for you, for I will accept his prayer not to deal with you according to your folly" . . . So Eliphaz the Temanite and Bildad the Shuhite and Zophar the Naamethite went and did what the Lord told them; and the Lord accepted Job's prayer' (Job 42.7, 9). I asked Kevork whether sense could be made of this turn in events in the Book of Job. What qualified Job the accuser of God to be an intercessor in prayer for his friends who had come vehemently to a defence of the divine justice? Kevork did not have to think long. Job the righteous one had suffered. It was his suffering which had qualified him. And Kevork drew the connection with Jesus's suffering and death on the cross. Out of his pain and affliction, a modern Job living in the ruins of his old life had discovered the redemptive meaning of his personal suffering and the suffering of his people.

The Bible has no foolproof answer for suffering. Rather, it confirms what human experience already knows – that suffering is an enduring part of human existence. Nevertheless, in the gospel of Jesus Christ, God gives us the hope that all of our suffering in some profound, deep sense has purpose and is ended in Jesus Christ. This is St Paul's answer ultimately when he writes in his Letter to the Romans, 'He who did not spare his own Son but gave him up for us all, will he not also give us all things with him?' (Rom. 8.32).

An Armenian theology of the cross

Perhaps no one in Armenian theology better expressed the necessity of the cross for salvation than the sixth-century theologian and philosopher David the Invincible. In his 'Encomium of the Holy Cross of God', David quoted St Paul in Galatians 3.1, 'Almost before your eyes was Jesus Christ shown as ascended on the Cross.' He then admonished his reader, 'But you think differently because you do not want to follow the Cross. For where [the] Cross, there the Crucified; and where Cross and Crucified, there Crucifixion.' Yet this is the great paradox and promise of Christian faith, that through death on the cross salvation is accomplished. 'Now therefore, when we say Cross, we here mean Golgotha, and here is crucifixion, here is sacrifice, and through it redemption.'[4]

For David, 'the Cross is the Cross of God, and He Himself, the Crucified One, God immortal, uncircumscribable and infinite'. This, he insists, is the summing up of all Christian belief in salvation and of all Christian hope. All of our brokenness, all of our guilt, all of our suffering and even dying is taken up and overcome once and for all by the immortal One nailed to the cross. Here is the true victory of the cross. David concludes, 'Henceforth, he who worthily embraces the Cross and communes with it does not do so with a mere cross, but evidently with the awesome power itself of God crucified on it.'[5]

Christian theologians have argued that there is a need for a restoration of the image of God in the light of the awful dimensions of human slaughter and ecological destruction in our time. This need for a restoration of the image of God certainly holds true for Armenian theology and the Armenian church after the genocide. Armenians must recover Christ in his humility, suffering and compassion on the cross. In the words of David the Invincible, 'Now he who laid Himself down indeed did so through and on the Cross. And he who gave Himself on it is still on it and does not distance Himself from it.' Christ is on the cross for everlasting. There is no other

Christ and Saviour than the Christ-nailed-on-the-Cross. And he is with us
in life and death. 'He who truly died, the same is ever living.'[6]

Yes, on the cross Christ defeated Satan and death. But that victory came
at a price. The church as that community which is, for ever, called to
remember the cross and live the form of Christ must also be willing to pay
the price. The Armenian genocide and its legacy stand as tragic reminders
that the redemptive worth of the Armenian church depends more than ever
upon its living a sacrificial and cruciform existence. We must never forget
that Jesus even after the resurrection bore the marks of the nails on his
hands and the gash of the spear which pierced his side. On the cross the
immortal Son experienced human pain and affliction and took it with him
into the life of God for ever. We not only know the incarnate Son of God as
co-sufferer with us but, in turn, as the people of God, we grieve in the
Spirit with the Father over the desolation of our fellow human beings. The
time has come for my church to abandon its mediaeval triumphalism and to
strip itself of its gilded vestments and expose its wounds which are Christ's,
which it bears for the sake of the afflicted. The Armenian church must be a
church whose compassion rests upon the knowledge and experience of the
affliction of its children. Only in this way is the church truly Christ's
imitator as well as his benefactor. Only in this way will the painful memory
of genocide be replaced with the joyful experience of Christ's living
presence.

Like Christ, the church must be the good Samaritan who helps the
wounded person on the road. But the wounded stranger must also be seen
as Christ himself. The church must come to his aid wherever he is to be
found. For as Christ commands and as he promises: 'Come, you that are
blessed by the Father, inherit the kingdom prepared for you from the
foundation of the world; for I was hungry and you gave me food, I was
thirsty and you gave me something to drink, I was a stranger and you
welcomed me, I was naked and you gave me clothing, I was sick and you
cared for me, I was in prison and you visited me . . . Truly I tell you, just
as you did it to one of the least of these who are members of my family, you
did it to me' (Matt. 25.34–36, 40).

I earnestly hope that the Armenian church – and that ultimately means
all who comprise it, clergy and laity alike – will make the Armenian
genocide a redemptive memory. May the church behave as the co-suffering
body of Christ among the afflicted, friend and stranger alike, and take the
confident step, in the light of Christ's victory on the cross, to be a ministry
of intercession, reconciliation and healing in a violent and despairing
world. For, as St Paul said: 'Neither death, nor life, nor angels, nor

principalities, nor things present, nor things to come, nor height nor
depth, nor anything else in all creation shall be able to separate us from the
love of God, which is in Christ Jesus our Lord' (Romans 8.38–39).

Notes

1. D. Miller and L. Tourian Miller, 'An Oral History Perspective on Responses to
the Armenian Genocide', in *The Armenian Genocide in Perspective*, ed.
R. Hovannisian, New Brunswick, New Jersey 1986, 194.

2. B. Carlson, 'The Children of Armenia', *Northeast (The Hartford Courant)*, 14
May 1989, 16.

3. E. Berkovits, *Faith after the Holocaust*, New York 1973, 127.

4. A. Sanjian, (ed.), *David Anhaght: The Invincible Philosopher*, Atlanta, Georgia
1986, 88.

5. Ibid., 87, 86.

6. Ibid., 85, 87.

Dead but Still Missing: Mothers of Plaza de Mayo Transform Argentina

Mary E. Hunt

Marcha a Plaza de Mayo

Formemos compañeras
que nuestra hora es
pongamos los emblemas
Amor-Justicia-Paz.

Marchemos todas juntas
marchemos sin cesar
la ronda de las Madres
pronto va comenzar.

Ya vuelan las palomas
que en su revoloteo
apoyan nuestras penas
en un simbolo de Paz.

Entremos compañeras
a la ronda del pesar
y como es este letargo
de nuestro esperar.

Con el pañeulo blanco
en un gran silencio
pidamos con angustia
¡Piedad Dios Piedad!

. . .

Reneuva la esperanza
pues ellos volverán
igual que las palomas
su sitio han de ocupar.

Y cuando nos alejamos
oimos en el espacio
los ecos de las voces
clamando ¿dónde estan . . . ?

Magdalena¹

Introduction

The Mothers of Plaza de Mayo in Argentina are an international symbol of resistance, grassroots organizing, and the triumph of the weakest, most vulnerable members of society over powerful forces. Their fidelity to their children who allegedly were 'disappeared' by military forces, and their remarkable courage in the face of dangerous repression, mark them as an outstanding example of the common human effort to survive personally and through one's offspring.

That most of their children were never found, and that many of their grandchildren will never be known to them, does not diminish the impact of their actions. To the contrary, their persistence despite the clear and constant negation by government officials of their demands only makes them all the more salutary in the face of mass death. In this article I focus on the symbols and images which the Mothers generated and are, reflecting on their contribution to an ecumenical theology of death albeit in a Catholic context.

I worked in Argentina as a Frontier Intern from 1980–1981, teaching theology at the ecumenical seminary (ISEDET) and working with women's groups through the Centro de Estudios Cristianos. Because human rights work was such a crying need, I became involved with Servicio Paz y Justicia under the direction of Adolfo Perez Esquivel (Nobel Peace Prize winner, 1980) which was closely allied with the Madres de Plaza de Mayo. Every Thursday afternoon at 3:30 I was privileged to join the groups in silent march around the Plaza de Mayo, a large public square in front of the Casa Rosada, the main government office building in the heart of Buenos Aires.

One day in 1981, marching with two Mothers on my arms, I was struck by their comments. One, in a lovely velvet jacket, said 'Oh, you look just like my daughter who disappeared.' The other, in an old faded sweater, added, 'My daughter was about your age when she disappeared. She, too, was involved in social change.' Having just turned thirty and being justifiably frightened by the danger we were in, I felt the awesome impact when integrity, imagination, organization and despair come together. These women, who had lost their children, had nothing more precious to lose. Their all-out efforts, to the point of death and disappearance for even some of them, left no doubt in my mind that Love-Justice-Peace are preconditions for humanity. I learned that people will actualize them under the most barbarous circumstances, or die trying, an important lesson in the ways of the human spirit.

History

The Mothers de Plaza de Mayo formed in 1977 during a brutal period of

Argentine history.[2] Nearly a century of alternating military and civilian governments, the rise and fall of General Peron, an economy held hostage to whopping inflation, and the eventual declaration of a state of emergency on 6 November 1972 followed by the military coup on 24 March 1976, issued in unprecedented repression. When the military dictatorship was finally ended on 10 December 1983 with the election of President Raul Alfonsin, more than 30,000 people had been detained or 'disappeared' in the name of restoring 'order and decency'.

Most of those who disappeared were young people, overwhelmingly university students and social activists. Jews were taken in numbers that vastly outweighed their percentage in the population. Women made up 30% of the lost, with 3% of them reported to have been pregnant at the time they were taken, hence the later concern of the Grandmothers of Plaza de Mayo to find their children's children through forensic investigations. Even high school students were abducted, an infamous case being the so-called 'Night of the Pencils', 16 September 1976, when sixteen, one could call them children, were taken from the city of La Plata. More than 100 journalists were taken, some for making public the very symbols of repression, like the Ford Falcons, the unmarked cars of the military who would swoop upon a house and make off with their prey.

It was as a collective response to this unspeakable horror that nine women, under threat of accusation for 'illicit association', which carried a stiff jail sentence, got together to petition President Videla for the whereabouts and return of their disappeared children. They were all mothers, hence their name, and their meeting place was the most famous city square. Plaza de Mayo.

As the Mothers tell it, they were so naive and politically unsophisticated that they gathered first on Saturday, forgetting that the president's schedule was Monday through Friday. Then they thought about Friday but decided it was an unlucky day. Finally they decided on Thursday at 3:30 p.m., and the day and time have been sacred ever since. The Mothers were immediately dubbed 'Las Locas', the crazy women, but over the years, as the logic and urgency of their message became increasingly obvious, the nickname fell away and everyone called them simply 'Las Madres'.

On Mother's Day, 5 October 1977, they published an advertisement in a local newspaper with their names and identity card numbers, 237 strong. They implored: 'The most cruel torture for a mother is uncertainty about the destiny of her children. We ask for a legal process to determine their innocence or guilt.' Other groups, notably the Centre for Legal and Social

Studies (CELS, Centro de Estudios Legales y Sociales) and the
Permanent Assembly of Human Rights (APDH, Assemblea Permanente
de Derechos Humanos), were already in action, but the Mothers focused
on their being women in a macho society, mothers in a Catholic culture,
and activitsts in a country in which women had only had the right to vote
for two decades. They always insisted on the right of the children to fair
trials, not simply proclaiming their innocence but underscoring that it was
the act of 'disappearing' them, not even granting them the dignity of a
death and burial, that magnified the crimes.

The small band grew, Thursday after Thursday, when, at the stroke of
3:30, dozens, then hundreds, of women would materialize from the
crowded downtown sidewalks, discreetly slip on their trademark white
handkerchiefs, and process in silent vigil for thirty minutes when, just as
effectively, they would disperse into the crowd again. Police surveillance
and harassment were constant. Armed officers on horseback or with buses
waited on the four corners of the Plaza. Plainclothes police, including a
number of women, would sit on the benches and watch, photograph,
sometimes even infiltrate the marches. Husbands and compañeros were
also on the sidelines, this being a women's protest, though in later years
they, too, joined the procession. More than fifty Mothers were arrested in
January 1979, and some were actually disappeared. Despite differences in
age, class and ethnic background, the Mothers banded together in
common cause.

The Mothers used every means at their disposition: the press,
international pressure, demonstrations, political manoeuvring, coalition
building, through the period of the Proceso, the Malvinas War in 1982 and
on through the period of democratization, from 1983 to the present (1992).
In 1983, during its waning days, the Junta, the military ruling group,
published its infamous attempt to exonerate itself of all blame by claiming
that those who disappeared were terrorists, and that they were killed for
the security of the nation.

Final details of the whereabouts of the children were never forthcoming,
though it is widely believed that many of them were tortured, killed and
buried in NN (no name) graves, or, in some cases, thrown from airplanes
into the Rio de la Plata which separates Argentina from Uruquay, from
such a height and at such a velocity as to have the bodies disintegrate on
impact.

For the Mothers, the struggle was not over despite the good news of
democracy in 1983. Hebe de Bonafini, a long-time leader of the group,
announced that instead of demanding an accounting from the military

government, the Mothers would simply turn their attention to the civilian elected officials. Their claim was 'Aparicion con vida', in essence, that their children had been taken away alive and that they wanted them back alive. Of course this was a controversial call, as many families, desperate for some resolution to the horrors they had lived through, simply took the government's word that their children had been killed.

Details were left aside and the results of a government study group (CONADEP, National Commission of Disappeared People) were less than satisfactory since so many important issues were thought to have been swept under the rug. But for a civilian government anxious to move on, this was the unhappy solution. The Mothers actually split into two groups in 1986 over strategies in the face of these government actions and over related internal matters. Government efforts to put this bloody chapter behind it complicated the dynamics and exhausted the already devastated family members. In a series of controversial moves in late 1986 and 1987, President Alfonsin and the Supreme Court effectively stopped procedures against many active-duty officers, claiming that most were simply following orders.

This virtual amnesty ended an era, but the Mothers remain active in Argentine social and political life; they work with women's and lesbian-gay groups to open Argentine society to the diverse dimensions of late-twentieth-century life. Their continued weekly marches are a testimony to the memory of their children, and moreover a guard against the same cycle beginning again. Their refusal to take the government's answer, though futile in the ways of coalition politics, is a vibrant example of women's barrier-breaking and insistence on truth. They may not have succeeded in bringing back their children, but they have managed against formidable odds to replace people with living symbols, to move from individual children to community response, and to stake out a place in the history of human struggle.

Symbols and interpretations

The Mothers are a wealth of symbols. First, their gender and status as mothers is confounding and contradictory. Argentina is as patriarchal a society as one can imagine, with women's roles in society sharply curtailed, still, despite an active feminist movement for nearly two decades, with expectations of 'good wife and mother' at home preparing the meals. Las Madres were quick to say that they aimed to accomplish what their men could not, namely, to confront the government out of their anguish and necessity as mothers. In an overwhelmingly Catholic country, the role of the mother, indeed based on Mary in the form of Our Lady of Lujan as patron saint of the armed forces, is central. They honoured this reality and transformed it at the same time. Death does that to life.

Second, the women chose the white handkerchief as their symbol. At first it was a plain, simple piece of cloth, something every woman would own and some women would whip out to cover their heads to enter a church or to guard against the rain. Later they began to embroider and/or write on the handkerchiefs the names and dates of the birth and disappearance of their children, turning the handkerchief into the tombstone the disappeared would never have. After all, the worst part of their suffering was articulated by the father of one of the disappeared: 'the absence of a body to mourn is the indescribable agony of this never ending drama'.[3]

A third symbol was the circle, the slow, steady, unchanging route in front of the Casa Rosada. The women did not choose a straight-line march, a face-to-face confrontation with power. Instead, they spoke loudly in their silent, predictable rounds, fairly etching into the sidewalk the truth of their claims. Later they added speeches, but only years after they had hallowed the ground with their indomitable presence.

Another symbol the women used was silhouettes painted on sidewalks all over the city. I will not forget awakening one morning in late 1983 just before the inauguration of President Alfonsin to find the city inundated with chalk figures, including pregnant women with fetuses visible. The dead had returned, but they were still missing.

Yet another time, the Mothers adorned the city and especially their offices with cut out hands linked together like children's paper dolls. The hands were a double-edged symbol, of those who were gone as well as those who were linked in seeking their return. Their symbols never gave in to the reality of death; rather, held out for the necessity of truth.

Words carried power. Newspapers were key in spreading the message, but some self-censored in compliance with government pressure. Poetry proliferated about the disappeared as Mothers wrote their 'songs of life, love and liberty'.[4] Some of the survivors even wrote poetry and prose about their experiences, notably Jacobo Timerman and Alicia Partnoy.[5] Protest signs and banners became a genre all their own with murals of the disappeared plastered all over the city.

Photographs of the disappeared children became common sights in the Plaza. Some Mothers even attached them to their handkerchiefs or wore them as large sandwich signs, a poignant sign of their desperation and their hope. They kept their children nearby in pictures in their living rooms and by their beds. Photographs of the Mothers, including photographs of the Mothers with the photographs of their children, helped to make them into the recognizable symbol they are now and helped other women in struggle to emulate them, kerchiefs and all. As Marjorie Agosin observed: 'The photographs stopped being a means of generating hallucination or mere signs that record the seasons of feeble times. They existed as witnesses to the immediacy of history.'[6]

The dove became a symbol for many of the Mothers. This traditional symbol of peace was conflated with the pigeons which feed on Plaza de Mayo, birds all flying as freely as the Mothers wanted their children to live. The dove was the most explicitly religious symbol, the closest to the Catholic background of most of the women, but the church-based meaning was avoided because the church avoided the Mothers.

The church as an institution was at best ambivalent on the question of the disappeared. Several high officials distinguished themselves as part of the resistance, and the Mothers managed a brief audience with the Pope. A few parish churches became meeting places when the Mothers were in grave physical danger. But for the most part the Argentine hierarchy and the Vatican diplomats were seemingly immune to the pleas of the women for help. Likewise, a painful symbol was the huge cathedral of Buenos Aires locked many a Thursday afternoon when the Mothers could well have used it as a haven from the police tear gas.

Argentina may be overwhelmingly Catholic, but Jewish, Protestant and other religious people, along with the stalwart left (if unpopular to the hierarchy Catholic), formed groups like the Ecumenical Movement for Human Rights (MEDH) to bring about justice. Happily, in these circles there was sensitivity to the interfaith dimensions of the problems and proposed solutions, not an over reliance on the Catholic Church.

Conclusion

The Mothers reflect best on their own situation, why they acted and what it means to them. Hebe de Bonafini captures the essence: 'The woman I was before gave me the preparation, the maternal feelings and the tenderness to be the woman I am today, because in spite of the fact that I'm a very tough person, some people say like a "warm rock", we never separate our feelings, our tenderness, the human part, from the politics.'[7]

They never claimed to be explicitly feminist, yet they understood their symbolic and real power as women. They never traded on motherhood as

sentiment, rather on parenthood, indeed adulthood, as the responsibility to see to the care and nurture of future generations. Nor did they ever shrink from the inexplicable ravaging of an entire generation: 'We will never accept they are dead until those responsible are punished . . . They can't negotiate with the blood of our children.'[8]

This is a group, representing hundreds of thousands of Argentines, that did not formulate a creed nor a canon. Rather, they stood firm for their children, hence for themselves, in divine defiance of death without bodies.

Notes

1. Magdalena in *Cantos de Vida, Amor y Libertad*, Madres de Plaza de Mayo, Buenos Aires 1984, 174–5. I have deliberately left this song untranslated. Its meaning and spirit will be evident from what follows.
2. A full historical analysis is beyond the scope of this article, but a comprehensive overview of the situation can be found in Jo Fisher, *Mothers of the Disappeared*, Boston 1989, especially 11–31.
3. Emilio F. Mignone, Preface to *Circles of Madness: Mothers of the Plaza de Mayo*, by Marjorie Agosin with photographs by Alicia d'Amico and Alicia Sanguinetti, Fredonia, NY 1992.
4. Cf. note 1.
5. Cf. Jacobo Timerman, *Prisoner without a Name, Cell without a Number*, New York 1981, and Alicia Partnoy, *The Little Schoolhouse*, Pittsburgh, PA 1986.
6. Marjorie Agosin, *Circles of Madness* (n. 3), 1.
7. Hebe de Bonafini, quoted in *Mothers of the Disappeared* (n. 2), 158.
8. Ibid.

The Dissonant Sounds of Hope: The Music of Mass Death and Christian Liturgical Remembrance

Richard N. Fragomeni

In this article it is asked whether twentieth-century Euro-American music, composed to commemorate the victims of mass death, offers significant insights to Christians who keep the memory of the passion of Christ in liturgical gatherings. To this purpose, the history of the music of mass death will first be outlined. Then, one specific composition of this genre will be described in some detail. Finally, some conclusions will be drawn about insights which this musical genre offers to Christian celebration.

The musical memory of the dead

The repertoire of Euro-American music includes a vast collection of elegiac compositions that commemorate the dead. Within this collection, the distinction is often made between liturgical music and sacred music. The liturgical music of this genre, beginning with the plainchant setting of the Latin requiem mass, and including the compositions of Dufay, Ockeghem and Palestrina, to name a few, was intended to be used within the Roman liturgy for the dead, both at the time of burial and on the occasion of the commonly celebrated *missa pro defunctis*.

Sacred or religious music, on the other hand, while drawing its inspiration and, in many cases, its texts from liturgical music for the dead, was composed primarily to commemorate the memory of the departed in the concert hall or church, where no accompanying liturgical ritual was enacted. The *Requiems* of Mozart, Brahms or Verdi, for instance, are sacred compositions. From the perspective of present liturgical standards, these sacred works could not be performed within the liturgy without considerable violation to the norms of current liturgical practice. While this distinction is important, the interrelatedness of both liturgical and sacred compositions for the dead in text, form and aspiration is not to be forgotten.

In this article our attention will primarily focus on sacred music composed to commemorate mass death and the insights such public auditory memory offers to liturgical remembrance.

When we examine the sacred music for the dead we can note two general features of these compositions. First, the texts and movements of the musical works are generally taken directly from liturgical or biblical sources, or are inspired by them. Secondly, until the twentieth century, the sacred music for the dead was commonly composed to honour a patron or a friend of the musician. For instance, Verdi's operatic *Requiem*, sometimes called the 'Manzoni Requiem', directly follows the mass parts of the Roman liturgy for the dead and is dedicated to Alessandro Manzoni, the author of *I Promessi Sposi*, and a close personal friend of the composer.

In the twentieth century the sacred music of death takes what seems to be a new turn in orientation and style. It features requiem compositions written specifically to commemorate victims of war, violence and disease, employing both sacred and secular texts to speak of the agony of human hostility and pain. This music can be called the music of mass death.

This genre of music first occurs in the requiems and in the music of mourning composed to commemorate the fallen soldiers of the First World War. In England, for instance, there were the compositions of Elgar, Bliss, Foulds and Delius, creating musical works to commemorate dead soldiers. Delius's work, composed between 1914–1916, and entitled *A Pagan Requiem*, is dedicated to the memory of all young artists who had fallen in the first Great War. J. C. Foulds wrote *A World Requiem* in 1923 in memory of the military dead.

Probably the best known music of mass death from this century was composed after World War II. The *War Requiem* of Benjamin Britten is considered the classic in this genre. Britten composed this work for the dedication of the new cathedral of St Michael's in the English city of Coventry. This new cathedral is built upon the ruins of the original edifice, destroyed by bombing in the Second World War. The new cathedral stands amidst the ruins of the old, as a memorial to the atrocities of human warfare.

War Requiem was first performed on 30 May 1962 in the new cathedral. It is a musical work of great poignancy, composed around the textual material of both the Latin requiem mass and the anti-war poems written in English by the British poet Wilfred Owen, a soldier and victim of the First World War. The tension of meaning created between the Latin texts of eternal rest and the anti-war texts of the poetry is brought forward musically by the interchange of solo voices, boys choir, adult chorus and full orchestra.

Of musical importance is Britten's use of the tritone, or the tonal interval of three whole steps. In the Middle Ages, this tonality was known as the *diabolus in musica*, the forbidden tone in musical composition; Britten exploited this interval to underscore the demonic despair of war.

The intertextual tension of meaning and music is resolved at the conclusion of the work, when both the poetry of Owen and the texts of the requiem mass plead for eternal peace and the end of senseless carnage. In keeping the memory of the atrocity of war and all its victims, Britten inscribed this composition to the memory of four friends killed in World War II.

Britten's work most clearly alerts us to a vast array of Euro-American music of mass death. Musical compositions have been written to commemorate the mass slaughter of those who have died in Nazi concentration camps and in the fires of Hiroshima. The agonies of the Vietnam War and Chernobyl have also prompted musical memorial. For instance, *The Third Symphony* of Leonard Bernstein, known as the 'Kaddish Symphony', and Arnold Schoenberg's *A Survivor from Warsaw* commemorate the victims of the Holocaust. The music of Nancy Van de Vate, especially her *Krakow Concerto*, does the same, while her *Chernobyl* keeps the memory of victims of the nuclear spill. The *Rock Requiem*, a little known work by the United States composer Lalo Schiffrin, was composed in memory of the victims of the Vietnam War.

Also beginning to appear in this century are musical compositions commemorating the dead of the AIDS epidemic. This music seeks to keep alive the memory of the nameless casualties of the disease. It attempts to alert its hearers to the fact that not unlike war, AIDS is not an event of the past, but an occurrence that continues to take its toll of human life. The *First Symphony* of John Corigliano, for example, commissioned for the centennial of the Chicago Symphony Orchestra, was inspired by the death of several of his friends with AIDS. The movements of the symphony are dedicated to their memory so that in the midst of the anonymous numbers who have died of AIDS, the names of a few will keep alive the names of many.

Among the twentieth-century Euro-American composers of the music of mass death, the work of Krzysztof Penderecki is of special importance to the topic of this article. Serious works of Penderecki are notably dedicated to the memory of the victims of mass death and are representative of this genre. His work can offer a focus to our conversation and a matrix for the insights which this genre bears for Christian liturgy.

Krzysztof Penderecki and the music of mass death

The Polish born Krzysztof Penderecki (b. 1933) is an orchestral, choral and operatic composer of formidable skill and musical imagination. Penderecki's music, needless to say, receives varied reviews from musical critics because of the challenging form and style of his musical compositions.

Penderecki's many choral compositions, employing a vast array of new timbres, include the *Passio et Mors Domini Nosti Jesu Christi secundum Lucam* (1966), *Dies Irae*, an oratorio in memory of the victims of Auschwitz (1967), *The Utrenya I: The Entombment of Christ* (1969–1970), *The Utrenya II: The Resurrection* (1971), and the *Polish Requiem* (1980–1984).

The oratorio *Dies Irae* offers an articulate illustration of the genre of the music of mass death. To limit our discussion in this article an examination of this work will be helpful.

This short oratorio, whose performance time is approximately twenty-four minutes, is dedicated to the memory of the victims murdered in Auschwitz. Its title, *Dies Irae*, the day of wrath, is taken from the traditional sequence from the mass for the dead of the Roman liturgy. The liturgical text most likely has its origins in an ancient Advent hymn of eschatological hope.

The oratorio was finally completed in 1967 when Penderecki was thirty-four years old. It was commissioned to be part of the dedication ceremony for the unveiling of a monument commemorating the victims of the extermination in the concentration camp of Auschwitz-Birkenau in Poland.

The oratorio is a blend of strong texts and extreme dissonances of timbre and harmony, quite novel to the ears of its original listeners. The text of the oratorio, while named after a movement of the traditional mass for the dead, does not follow the traditional form of the sequence of the requiem mass. Rather, it is a catenation of texts, chosen by Penderecki from a variety of sources. These sources include texts from the Bible, from Greek literature, and from contemporary French and Polish poetry. As one listens to the oratorio, the fabric of the text is tightly woven as one piece. Psalm 116, Paul's First Letter to the Corinthians, the Book of Revelation, Aeschylus' tragedy *The Eumenides*, and the poetry of Wladyslaw Broniewski, Tadeusz Rozewicz, Louis Aragon and Paul Valéry are linked together with great artistry. Penderecki had the texts translated into Latin for the libretto of the oratorio, keeping in its original language only the Greek of Aeschylus. The use of Latin and Greek add a haunting and archetypal dimension to the texts and bring a solemnity to the overall sense of the sound.

According to the programme notes of the performance, the instrumentation of the oratorio is quite unusual. The work calls for an orchestra with neither violins nor violas, only cellos and double basses. Three saxophones replace the clarinets, and the percussion section is quite extensive. The large mixed chorus becomes the foundation of the musical sound and at times is divided into twenty-four parts. The chorus is joined by three soloists, soprano, tenor and bass, who are featured throughout the work. Penderecki uses this array of instrumentation and voices to create an inescapable sound which surrounds the listener with the terror of the Holocaust memory it seeks to commemorate.

The oratorio is in three sections, bearing the titles *Lamentatio*, *Apocalypsis* and *Apotheosis*. The first section, *Lamentatio*, begins with the text of Psalm 116, 'The snares of death are around me', and continues by featuring the soprano soloist singing the poetry of Broniewski, which begins with the words *corpora parvulorum*, that is, the bodies of children, an image heard throughout the oratorio. Taking the direction from its title, this first section is, indeed, a lamentation for the bodies of children, bodies with wounds, bodies of boys and girls whose youth was robbed in death. These memories are kept in the dissonance of the sound of chorus and orchestra. The chorus, for instance, movingly recalls the memory of childhood destroyed by brutal death with the lines of Rozewicz as the orchestra ominously paints a foreboding tone:

> In huge crates
> Dry hair-tufts billow
> Of strangled people,
> And a small braid,
> A pigtail with a ribbon
> Pulled in a class-room
> By naughty boys.

The second movement, *Apocalypsis*, features the bass soloist. It juxtaposes texts from the Book of Revelation and *The Eumenides*. This section speaks of beasts and humans being burned alive in the apocalyptic scenes of judgment and horror. The section rises to its crescendo and speaks the terror of the memory being recalled by employing the sound of an air-raid siren and the rattling of chains and the shaking of a thunder-sheet. These sounds are a form of tone painting which offer a force of music to the already horror-making imagery of the text.

The third section begins with the words *absorpta est mors in victoria* from I Corinthians 15, accompanied by the ringing of a single chime. This section, entitled *Apotheosis*, brings the work to a close in dramatic fashion. The texts speak of the swallowing up of death in victory and continue with the vision of a new heaven and earth from the Book of Revelation. Paul Valéry's words, 'The winds rise! . . . Let us try to live!', are woven into the section, underlining the message of hope and transfiguration. However, the closing words heard in the oratorio are again a tragic reminder of the death of children, as the chorus echoes for one last time the phrase used throughout the work, *corpora parvulorum*, offering a not too certain surety to hope.

The overall effect of this atonal and dissonant composition continues to be quite shattering, even to ears accustomed to hearing twentieth-century experiments in musical timbre. Penderecki's use of quarter-tones, angular intervals for soloists and chorus, the extremes of dynamics and the colouring of orchestral sounds, gives the oratorio its haunting character. It is a highly evocative work, which refuses to relinquish its goal of keeping the voices of the victims alive in our ears. This particular instance of the music of mass death speaks the memories of the dead in new tonalities, so that the death of the masses does not degenerate into the platitudinous. The agony of children becomes the memory from which this oratorio forms the new expression of hope. The music deals with this anguish in sounds and texts that clamour for the response of the heart.

Dies Irae, as representative of the music of mass death, allows us to make four general observations about this musical genre. First, the music of mass death is a form of public memory that invites listeners into the shared event of pain and the useless human suffering of vast populations. It does this by the combination of sound and in most cases texts which speak of the horror of war and human violence.

Second, it is music that compels us to remember and to lament as a community in communion with the dead, rather than simply inviting us to listen passively to the woes of others in their mourning. It seems that the goal of this music of mass death is to achieve a tensive interplay between sound and texts, bringing to life the forgotten and nameless multitude; bringing the dead to life in the power of sound.

Third, the texts which this genre of music employs are those of lamentation and hope. The texts chosen and written are strong statements of horror, which seek to change human perceptions and attitudes and to invite a solidarity with the dead so that together we might live in hope of a human future beyond the ravages of destruction. Linked to the sounds, timbres and atonality of twentieth-century music unfamiliar to the ears of many listeners, the compositions are inescapable symbols of what has been and what can be.

Finally, the hope emerging from the lamentation of this music is not predestined, nor naively certain. It demands human transformation. As we see in the *Dies Irae*, the bodies of children still cry out. In our hope, the music demands a response, lest we forget, and lest our hope becomes complacent acceptance of the cycles of decline.

The insights of the music of mass death for Christian memorial

This article has offered an outline of twentieth-century Euro-American music which has been composed to commemorate the victims of mass death. Employing the specific example of Penderecki's *Dies Irae*, the conversation now explores three insights which this musical genre offers to those who commemorate the passion of Christ at liturgical gatherings.

One important insight offered by this genre of music is the reminder that Christian liturgy is indeed a public memory of a community of faith. The liturgy is a memorial of the death of Christ and must include the remembrance of all victims. Folded into the memory of the crucified one, countless unnamed persons are given name and memory. In this memory of victims Christian liturgy does not operate in a cultural vacuum, and cannot see itself as separate from its cultural matrices. The work of keeping the memory of Christ and of enlivening the liberative energy which this memory has for human futures cannot be carried out by the liturgy alone. The liturgy needs cultural contexts of memory. The music of mass death offers to Christian memorial a significant portion of that context. Christians need to remember the influence which both Christian and Jewish liturgy has had upon it, so that it may become a mirror back to the community of the need for liberative memory and a cultural support to the transformation of the community of faith. Christian liturgy, like the music of mass death, must enhance and diffuse the awareness and the memory of mass human destruction, lest by forgetfulness the cross is reduced to the banal purpose of pendant jewellery. The music of mass death needs to be heard by Christians. It must be composed and encouraged as sacred music. In this, liturgy and sacred music of death can continually be mutually enhancing.

The importance of strong sounds and texts to activate human transformation is the second insight of this musical genre for Christian memorial. The strength of both the sounds and texts of the music of mass death offers overwhelming energies to the sympathetic imagination, so as to enter into solidarity with the dead. The sympathetic imagination is triggered by these compositions. It is this imagination in human consciousness which proffers the possibilities of interpreting reality in new ways of hope. The music of this genre refuses to deny the human possibility of devastation and destruction. In remembering with such force of sound and meaning, it invites the imagination to be transformed. In other words, the lamenting sound of this music prompts the sympathetic imagination to inhabit transformed worlds of peace, never forgetting the possibility of the distortions of power. As such, this music offers again the insight that the Christian liturgy must employ a strong language of revelation, a language that refuses to deny the voices of the voiceless. It is an invitation to the liturgy to craft texts that awaken the sympathetic imagination, lest the liturgy of the memorial of the death of Christ become a nostalgic plea to escape this world, or a prayer for an intervention from beyond, to forget the human mechanisms of destruction. It is an invitation to boldness.

A third insight comes from the innovative quality of the music of mass death. The genre takes older forms and texts and strains to discover the power of the memory it seeks to communicate by twisting a new sound and a new form of composition. To keep the memory of such atrocity, new forms and sounds must emerge from the cultural remnants of musical styles. In other words, the music of mass death draws from the cultural past and forges new sounds. The insight this offers to Christian liturgy awakens liturgical musicians to examine the cultural forms and sounds that are brought into the memorial of Christ's death. The musical antecedent for much of present Euro-American liturgical music is the love ballad, the jingle, the Broadway show tune. After such human atrocity, this musical style is too sweet-sounding to communicate the savage desecration of mass death.

The music of mass death invites Christian remembrance to a prophetic disclosure of grace. It impels Christians of every culture to be sensitive to the messages of art forms that prompt movements of communion and transformed human consciousness. It calls us to new musical and textual forms, so that both text and sound utter the explosive possibility of singing a new song to the Lord.

For Further Reading and Listening

Lawrence L. Langer, *Holocaust Testimonies: The Ruins of Memory*, New Haven, CT 1991.

Larry Mendes, 'Penderecki and Shostakovich: Death Affirms Life', *The Christian Century*, 18 March 1987, Vol. 104, 287–8.

Alec Robertson, *Requiem: Music of Mourning and Consolation*, London and New York 1968.

Wolfram Schwinger, *Krzysztof Penderecki: His Life and Work*, London 1989.

Recordings

Krzysztof Penderecki, *Dies Irae*, Compact Disc Digital Audio Recording CDCF 185, Conifer Records Limited 1990; *Polnisches Requiem*, Compact Disc Digital Audio Recording 429 721–2, Deutsche Grammophon 1990.

Commemorations

David N. Power

Mass death, or death by mass, often deprives its victims of human dignity in the way in which they die. It further deprives them of a face or a name attached to the accounts of their death or by which to be remembered.

In time of famine, those who die are surrounded by the struggle to survive. It is those who are weakest, who are least able to fend for themselves in obtaining the little whereby to keep alive, who are the first victims. In concentration camps, vestiges of human dignity and human choice are torn away from those held there well before the moment of death. In wars whose purpose is unclear to combatants, a sense of spiritual and moral abandon deprives death of dignity and haunts the survivors, making remembrance all the more difficult. When persons die from AIDS they are sometimes fortunate enough to have people to watch with them, but the prejudices of society and the refusal of many to associate with the ill lays a pall over their memory.

In all of these cases, as in others not mentioned, it is easier to get statistics than names of the dead. The events themselves are so shocking to human imagination that they are pushed into oblivion, together with the stories of those who died.

Nonetheless, in different parts of the world today there are those who are trying to establish not only immediate but long-term ways of commemorating the victims of catastrophe and tragedy. At times this is in the form of a monument of some sort, or of a story that has to be told to the children. Often enough, it is by way of keeping an annual commemoration. At Nagasaki and Hiroshima each year anniversary is kept of those who died from the explosion of the atomic bomb, and a tolling of bells in various parts of the world associates peoples of other nations with the memory of the dead.

The importance of actually naming the dead and of remembering the individual story, however many the victims, is illustrated by some commemorative events in the city of Washington in the United States of America. A wall has been erected there, in a hollow dug into the ground, close to the monuments to the memory of George Washington and Abraham Lincoln, which stand for the birth of the nation and the emancipation from slavery. By association with these monuments, the Vietnam Wall, as it is called, makes the event of the Vietnam conflict part of the national memory, however troublesome it be. It features the names of all who died. There are thus some 52,000 names carved into it, in the order determined by the date of each one's death, rather than in alphabetical order. Statistics give way to the actual record of names and dates. The monument has become almost a centre of pilgrimage, where people come from all over the country to keep faith with dead relatives or friends. They take rubbings of the names, place flowers and personal items (a letter, an old pair of boots, a photograph) by the wall, and stand in silent communion with the dead. At the time of year when commemoration is kept of war veterans, there is a reading of the names inscribed on the wall over several days. For this war, it is not enough to keep memory of those who died for their country, as with other wars; given the nature of the conflict, there is the desire to keep alive the fate and memory of each one. It is only in the individuality of the remembrance that the absurdity of the conflict can be overcome.

In October 1992, the memory of those who have died from AIDS was linked up with this monument, as with the other two national monuments, when a quilt covering thirteen acres of ground was spread close to it, on the land of the National Park of National Monuments. The quilt had over 20,000 panels, each dedicated to the memory of a person who had died from AIDS. Over a week-end, there was a continuous reading of their names over a public-address system and thousands came to remember, laughing and weeping their memories as they wandered between the panels of the quilt.

The commemorations invoked here do not of their nature include an appeal to Christian faith. They do, however, make the dead and the events by which they died part of the cultural and living memory of peoples. They have lessons to teach believers about keeping memory.

IV · Conclusions for Liturgical Remembrance

Calling Up the Dead

David N. Power

Jewish and Christian approaches to God have already been much affected by the remembrance of the Holocaust, the supreme example of senseless death and yet an event whose recall reshapes faith and hope in God. It has made us all think differently of human-incited death and of divine covenant. It raises special issues which have been considered in another number of *Concilium*.[1] Though therefore the Shoah is not in itself included among the topics for this volume, several of the authors refer to it. The questions that it raises, and the reactions that it evokes, provide background to what is asked about our response to multiple instances of mass death.[2]

Facing mass death

Events involving mass death raise more issues than those already raised by the simple fact of human mortality. Its causes engross and disturb as much as the fact of death itself. Apart from the tragedy of many lives abruptly cut short, the long-term effects on a community or society that witnesses this death are beyond calculation.

The situations described and the deaths recounted in this volume are vastly diverse in themselves. A common feature, however, is that in each case there is a tragedy in which not only the individual or even the family is affected, but the people or race or society is threatened. Besides finding a senselessness or an unaccountable evil in the way in which persons have died, it is asked whether in the light of this mass death there can be any future worthy of human beings. It is asked, too, what possible future there can be for those who die so senselessly.

One cannot equate death by human violence, death by war, death by genocide, death by disease, and death from natural disaster. Nonetheless, while mass death resulting from human violence has a particular note to it, in varying degrees the death brought on by natural calamities is not without an element of human responsibility. This is more so in some situations than in others. Famine resulting from drought, for example, becomes more catastrophic where unjust action, or political and economic interests, block a relief response or even contribute to the situation which brought on the famine in the first place. While death by natural disasters, such as flood or earthquake, may seem to stand out as a freak of nature, in today's world at least there is hardly any such situation where there is not a human failure involved. It may be this which causes people to have to live in conditions that make them vulnerable to the effects of flood (as in Bangladesh) or typhoons and earthquake (as in the Philippines), or it may be that the relief which could be given fails on account of human muddling, or worse still because of vested interests, economic, political and ethnic. Or it may be that humanity's careless exploitation of the environment has a part in the causes of natural disaster.[3]

Remembering the dead for the future

In the development of a human and Christian ethic, close analysis of situations in which mass death occurred or occurs is necessary in order to forge a global justice that addresses both its causes and its aggravating circumstances. While it is important to distinguish between earthly and human-made calamities, the need to face the issues of mass death in promoting a world-wide covenantal justice cannot be missed.[4]

This issue of *Concilium*, however, addresses this reality of mass death from an angle other than that of ethical deliberation. It asks how people face the tragedy, how they later remember it and how over time they commemorate the dead. Is it possible to retrieve from death the loss which affects both the living and the dead? In the wake of mass death, how does a people learn to look to a future when justice may be done to the dead as well as to the living? The ways of commemoration do not spell out the ethical solution, but they carry its seed in the vision offered or in the future conjured up in image. Remembering can carry a new potential for life in the remembrance of those who have perished.

One of the worst features of mass death is that persons disappear, as it were, without trace. Numbers are cited, names are difficult to garner. The very conditions under which people die are such that their dying is deprived of the features of the life-world which make even the decision to die, and dignified contact with others in dying, a human possibility.

From a fully human and Christian perspective, there can be no forgetting those who have disappeared in this way. They demand remembrance precisely because their lives were unrealized, cut short, and their dying forbidden its authentic expression of free, personal action. When names are obliterated in the massiveness of numbers counted or hazarded, these very names must be summoned up from the dead.

In so many situations of mass death the human factor that serves to bring it on has been the negation of the other as other, the refusal to live with the diversity of those who are other to the self.[5] Thus it is in the Armenian tragedy, in the disappearance of the opposition in Argentina, in what is termed ethnic cleansing in Bosnia, in the famines that are part of the economic North/South conflict, or in the ostracization of AIDS victims. The dead need to be brought back into living memory as the other who demands our recognition, if there is to be a future for all, living or dead, beyond this obliteration.

There seems in some quarters today to be an acute sensitivity to the senseless character of mass death and to the call to recognize the face of the other in the dead. Perhaps this is in part because of the kind of publicity which disaster receives in an age of global communication. More deeply it may be because the easy solutions proffered have faltered and failed. What countenance can be given to a philosophy optimistic of progress, or to a theology that appeals to divine providence and redemptive justice to explain senseless death? Similarly, after the wars of this century, with their monstrous weapons and unrestricted killing, there is little credibility to the patriotic slogan, *bonum est pro patria mori*.

In the reactions of different people and the efforts to get beyond such illusory answers, there is an endeavour to recover hope for the society or community which is violated by such massive or senseless death. Even while the social body as a whole must find its future, it is still to be recognized that the ability to overcome the evil depends on giving dignity to the individual. Respecting and remembering individuals in a way that defies the reduction to statistics, builds up the corporate hope. The corporate hope in turn redeems individuals, and redeems the times and the nothingness-in-time of those who are the victims of mass death. The ways in which people keep memorial are expressive of the endeavour to retrieve persons, to retrieve the race, not to let a culture die out, to promote a future, in short of the need to overcome death that appears absurd.

Springing up within communities and under the leadership of ritually sensitive persons, there is a creative appeal to story, symbol and ritual in the keeping of memory. There are multiple endeavours to find a response that emerges from the use of natural and cultural symbols, in rites, in commemorative monuments, in story, in music. This is vital to the future of humanity and to the solidarity between the living and the dead. It is from a cultural and symbolic creativity that lessons are learned of ways to remember disaster and to remain in communion with the dead.

The Christian perspective

Belief in God is called into question in face of mass death and in face of the question about what has happened to the dead. Prevailing images of God's action are distorted. This is not only on the basis of the questions which may arise about divine providence. More drastically, it has to do with what future God assures. God is called to issue in the promise of life to the nameless as well as to the named dead. There is no future possible in this world or in eternity without inclusion of those whose disappearing was without sense, even made deliberately senseless since they were counted dispensable.

For Christians witnessing the reality of mass death, there is an obscurity to what is promised in the covenant and in the resurrection of Jesus Christ. The inadequacy of traditional theological solutions has to be accepted. Paradoxically, where no explanation can be given, when the dead are commemorated the effort is not to find theological reasons for what has occurred but to retrieve the future in the light of eschatological promise.

This is where the memory of the passion and resurrection of Jesus Christ plays a vital role. The death of Jesus is remembered as the death for the other, to keep the other as other. The resurrection of Jesus is a promise for the future of life for all, and for a future in the solidarity of all who enter into life. It is also a promise that the past of all the dead can be taken up into the future of promise. This is not a mere assurance that all who die in the justice of God will have eternal life. It is a promise that out of their lives on earth, out of the apparent absurdity of their death, a future comes that belongs to the realization of covenant justice here on earth.

For Christians, memory is essentially eschatology. It takes from the past, it gives past to what has been simply non-past, to carry it forward to the future, indeed for the sake of the future. It includes a necessary affirmation of the other as other, and rejoices in the oneness with the self in the circuminsession of otherness. The affirming of the other is the way in which God is affirmed as absolute reality for the otherness and oneness of all, in death and beyond death.

Forging a corporate vision that gives a place in the future to the dead, even the individual dead, is the challenge which Christian worship picks up from the various examples discussed above. From a Christian perspective, this means a corporate eschatological vision, one that emerges from including the memory of the dead in the memory of Christ's pasch.

There have been times in history when reaction to disaster was apocalyptic. Soothsayers made predictions of the last times and looked to tragedy as a fiery divine judgment on the human enterprise. Christian hope, however, while it permits apocalyptic imagery to express a sense of divine judgment, is not apocalyptic in the sense of wiping out human history. It allows for a more just future on this earth, within the economic, political, cultural and religious mix which makes up the life-world. It is a hope that indeed looks ahead to some divinely given future when all are united in God's vision, but its immediate concern is for the rule of God here on earth. It envisages earthly societies that integrate hope for this earth with openness to the transcendental. It promotes an anamnestic solidarity that retrieves and redeems all the ages and all persons, however anonymous they were in their dying. The awesome challenge to faith and hope is not to leave the victims of mass or senseless dead to heavenly blessedness, but to give their memory, their names, their vitality, their promise, a place in the making of society and of a human world here and now.

Liturgy

As things have worked out in putting the volume together, its least developed part is that which is directly addressed to liturgies for the dead in face of mass death. That springs from the nature of things. In face of calamity, the efforts called forth are those needed to deal with the disaster and simply to dispose of bodies without creating further peril.

Even from those articles written about a Christian response in specific instances of mass death, it is clear enough that it is in non-liturgical services of one sort or another that anything approximating adequate memorial has occurred. There is little room for adequate ritual in the event itself, and worship books would appear callous were they to include an *editio typica* of rites for mass death. It must of necessity be in the longer rather than in the immediate aftermath of the event that commemoration be made. Each calamity will require its own particular response and its own particular commemoration. Nonetheless, some attention has to be given to liturgical ways of commemorating the victims of mass death, whether in the common rites of the church or in the rituals of local churches.

In fact as far as commemoration is concerned, the Shoah may again offer a paradigm, in the forms of its commemoration. The worship books of the Jewish people mark this remembrance with appropriate services. A number of inter-religious services have also been composed, in which Christians too take part, especially on the occasion of the Days of Remembrance.[6] As a Christian community, however, we do not have a memorial of this tragedy, even though Christians and humankind as such were deeply involved in it. We have no annual liturgy which impels congregations to take the challenge to hope of this event to heart.

This failure to look tragedy in the face is common enough in the celebration of the liturgy. It is as though we feared that hope would disappear were we to accept bewilderment over God's place in human affairs when they turn sour, or when simply reminding ourselves that humans are sinners does not answer the dilemma of such immense tragedy.

It is an odd fact that the church's calendar knows only triumphs, no tragedies. On 7 October, Lepanto is remembered but there is no red mark in our books for the black death, for the dead of the crusades, for the Jews who died in pogroms, or for the victims of wars. The only dead whom we remember annually are martyrs and saints, or once a year in a very generic way 'the holy souls'. For a long time, the church in Ireland kept memory of the dead of the famine of 1848 by the praying of the *De Profundis* at the end of every Mass, but that too disappeared with liturgical 'reforms'. Yet it is of those who died senselessly that there is in fact the greatest need to keep memory. If the Christian people lack in solidarity with these victims, Christian hope is a paltry thing.

On this score, our liturgical books could give some directives, mapping out some annual commemoration or forms that could be used with some regularity when events require a long-term remembrance. Though Christians keep alive their hope in the pasch of Christ, what this hope offers does not appear unless the heart is opened to the sorrow of non-sense, of life deprived, of death rendered inhuman and ignominious, of generations who lose their children, of peoples and countries whose future is jeopardized by its losses, not only personal but cultural. Penderecki wrote music to commemorate the dead of the concentration camps, so that it would keep on being played, with all its disturbing atonality. The Irish people kept on saying the *De Profundis* because as a people they still lived in the shadow of that terrible famine, their whole history and way of life having been twisted out of shape by it.

As mentioned several times, much human responsibility and sin is linked up with mass death. Worship therefore has to acknowledge sin and guilt. It may not, however, avoid the question of God's absence by, as it were, freeing God of responsibility, blaming the events in their totality on sin. They say something to the naming of God beyond seeing the divine as judge.

Liturgical elements

To end with some concrete suggestions, four things may be mentioned that belong to a liturgical remembrance of the victims of mass death that continues over time. *These have to do with marking the calendar, with giving voice to the dead, with repentance and with lament.*

The Calendar

These dead can be marked into the calendar, in much the same way as the Jewish people mark the annual remembrance of the Shoah.[7] When memories are renewed and the process of story and of naming continues, the sense of solidarity with the dead is revitalized through their inclusion. In devising a liturgy for this, much is to be learned from the rituals, the narrative, the poetry and from the music with which various cultures recall their victims.

Remembrance of the Shoah is, however, paradigmatic, and Jewish communities have invited Christian communities to share with them in this memory, recognizing its significance not only for Jewish people but for humanity as a whole. The services of these days dare to name the dread places where death was dealt out, such as Auschwitz and Dachau. They dare to revive religious memories of the covenant in the reading of Torah and in religious songs. They also dare to summon up personal memories, in stories left behind by the dead, or in their poems and drawings, all worked into memorial ritual.

Giving Voice to the Dead

The dead must be let speak within the liturgy, just as for example they speak from the wall of the monument to the dead of Vietnam in the city of Washington or from the wall of remembrance in Jerusalem, or in the readings from the death camps during the Days of Remembrance.

One specific Christian attempt to remember the dead of the concentration camps may give us pause, suggesting a litanic lament that serves as a model. When John Paul II went to Mauthausen, he stood before the ovens and cried out:

You people who have experienced fearful tortures – how worthy are you of the Lamentations of Jeremiah! What is your last word? Your word after so many years which separate our generation from the sufferings in the Mauthausen concentraton camp and in the many others?

You people of yesterday, and you people of today, if the system of extermination camps continues somewhere in the world even today, tell us, what message can our century convey to the next?

Tell us, in your great hurry, have we not forgotten your hell? Are we not extinguishing traces of great crimes in our memories and consciousness? . . .

Speak, you have the right to speak – you who suffered and lost your lives. We have the duty to listen to your testimony.[8]

This prayer expresses not only the enduring solidarity with the dead, not only the duty to remember them, but also the importance for all posterity to keep this memory as part of a living tradition.

In looking back to those who died in absurd wars, or to those who died in famine and in catastrophes of nature, Christian communities have to gather the recollections of the dead, in whatever form they are obtainable. Oral history sometimes serves, but it is a human and a Christian duty to cull this and set something of it in writing and in ritual, before it fades from living memory.

Repentance

There is frightful human evil at the root of much suffering and absurd death. There is likewise much self-centred interest that prevents attention to it, much complicity in what are the causes, and much silence and indifference in face of it. *In the Western world, to boot, there is the risk of trivializing it by the way in which catastrophes are recorded on television or in glossy magazines, alongside advertisements for food-stuffs or controversies about labelling food-packages in supermarkets.*

For this reason, confession of sin has to be integral to remembrance. This is not intended to encourage misplaced guilt. Nor is it intended to excuse God, as it were, by blaming all on humans, for the divine absence rests an enigma. Its aim is to bring to speech the depth of human sinfulness, not only that of the perpetrator, but even the sins of complicity and silence. It is by accepting a solidarity in sin that humans may come to a sense of solidarity in suffering. Out of this they may look for a common hope, for the living and the dead, in the quest for a saviour.

Lament

The voice of lamentation must ring out, the lamentation of the living and of the dead, flung into the pit. Lamentation does not simply bewail a situation and cry out in distress. It has the courage, born of dread, to wrestle with God's name and promise. It has the courage to dislodge God from the places in the human story that the creator and saving God has come to occupy. It dethrones those wisdoms about suffering and sin which appeal to the name of God. It is because those who lament dare to look away and to turn deaf ears to what is offered as consolation and comfort, or even judgment, that they are empowered to look again for God among the victims, in the throes of suffering and death. Jesus takes on the name of the just Abel, who cries with a loud voice from within our common agony, and from communion with the agony of the earth soiled with his blood. The promise of the resurrection of the Just One brings no theoretical answer but allows us in remembrance and eschatological hope to keep hoping, to gather even the nameless victims of senseless death into our common hope and horizon. It is a lamentation that holds to the vow of praise.

Conclusion

It is an hour in which Christian people must listen to those who dare to remember. Liturgy appropriates into the pasch of Christ all that emerges from the experience, the struggles, and the symbolic creativity of a people. Or else it continues its way, divorced from the cultural and symbolic matrix, appealing to anaemic symbolism and dead metaphors, immunizing the conscience against complaint, lament and vigorous remembrance. In failing to give voice to the horror aroused by massive death, it risks letting the dead bury their dead, and minimizes or trivializes the lives of all by its very failure.

Notes

1. See *The Holocaust as Interruption*, *Concilium* 175, April 1984.
2. This is made clear in the articles contributed to this issue of *Concilium* by Michel Deneken and Werner Jeanrond.
3. Semporé and De Mesa have both raised this question of tampering with the environment.
4. See the articles in *Christian Ethics and Economics in the North-South Conflict*, Part I, *Concilium* 140, December 1980.
5. See the paradigmatic reflections in Tzvetan Todorov, *La Conquête de l'Amérique*, Paris 1982.

6. Amongst others, see *Liturgies of the Holocaust*, ed. Marcia Sachs Littell, Lewiston and Queenston 1986.

7. See for example 'Service for Tish'a be-Av and Yom Hasho-ah', in *Gates of Prayer. The New Union Prayer Book*, New York 1975, 573–89, and 'Yom Ha-Shoah', in *Siddur Sim Shalom. A Prayerbook for Shabbat, Festivals, and Weekdays*, ed. Rabbi Jules Harlow, New York 1985, 828–43.

8. John Paul II, Address at Mauthausen, 24 June 1988, *Origins* 18, 1988, 124.

A World Catechism?

It is a trite remark to say that – especially in the Western world – we live at a time of deep crisis for faith. By that I do not mean the loss of all basic convictions, the loss of a belief that there is meaning in human life and death, the loss of an observance of ethical norms and values. Fortunately such basic convictions persist among a majority of men and women, even in the highly-secularized Western world. What I mean, rather, is the loss of the substance of that Christian faith which the church has presented to its faithful for centuries and a loss of positive 'knowledge' about what Christians should believe.

However, this situation is quite ambivalent. It is certainly to be regretted that many people, particularly among the younger generation, no longer have any knowledge of even the basic events of church history or of central elements of Christian life like the Lord's Prayer and the Ten Commandments. But should we regret that there are also other things that they no longer know? All those distorted ideas about sexual morality, all those mediaeval beliefs which prove too much for an enlightened awareness, like the Virgin Birth understood in biological terms, the bodily assumption of Mary into heaven understood in a naively physical way, or complicated theories on the divine Trinity?

Certainly we should do everything possible to ensure that the basic substance of the Christian faith is not lost among the younger generation. But should we necessarily mourn, shaking our heads over the decline in our culture, the passing of a casuistic morality and an over-complex dogmatics? Do we not need, rather, to be concerned to proclaim a basic and concentrated form of Christian faith, to reflect on its central elements as they are to be found in the New Testament? Such a basic and concentrated form of faith aims at achieving a Christian life in discipleship of Jesus Christ himself – through preaching, religious instruction, catechesis and theology. This is the need of the hour, in order to compensate for and catch up on the far-reaching loss of faith.

But how has Rome reacted? Has it seized the opportunity to introduce this basic and concentrated form of faith for a world church which is expressed in different cultures, nations and modes of thought? No, Rome has reacted in the way that a curial apparatus tends to react now. A plurality of Catholic theology is seen as a danger. The loss of faith is simply a negative phenomenon. And the world church is one uniform church under authoritarian leadership.

The only explanation for the presentation of a world catechism to the world church which is now taking place is a Roman anxiety at the loss of what is regarded in Rome as Catholic identity. But if one looks more closely, this catechism is more a Roman party catechism than a really Catholic world catechism. Even Vatican I (1871) refused to allow the Roman Curia, with its traditionalist theology, to ordain a catechism for the whole world. At that time the bishops recognized the danger that all cultures and traditions would be levelled out, that the legitimate Catholic plurality of the world church would be made uniform. Nor did anyone want that in Vatican II (1962–1965). But the Roman Curia has wanted it for a long time. Certainly this time the bishops had been asked for their views, but what was included in or omitted from the catechism was decided solely by a curial commission. In its old centralistic style, Rome is again seeking to impose its view of 'Catholicity'.

While much in this catechism is the common heritage of Catholicism, some new emphases can be recognized in its content. The Vatican does not find it difficult, for example, to expand the catalogue of sins and extend it to corruption, tax evasion, drunk-driving and a lack of respect for the environment. That is to be welcomed. But the decisive thing is that at other places where Rome should have shown the same insight, it does not do any rethinking but cements the old positions. That is true of questions like birth control and the prohibition of the remarriage of divorced persons, compulsory celibacy, the ordination of women and intercommunion. But it is also true of disputed dogmatic questions, from the primal state of paradise and the original sin of the first human couple, the fall of angels and the working of Satan in the world, and the appointment of the apostles at the Last Supper to be 'priests of the new covenant', to papal infallibility. All this is prescribed as irrevocable 'Catholic' teaching, heedless of the results of historical-critical exegesis, heedless of the theological discussion on these questions, heedless of the lack of acceptance by the majority of the faithful. Everything is backed up with endless quotations from the Bible, from councils, popes and theologians – all put on precisely the same level. In this way an attempt is made to turn a 'hierarchy of truths' into a 'truth of the hierarchy'.

But this catechism fits quite neatly into the conservative policy of the present Polish pope, under whose regime curial centralization and the Roman passion for regulation is having a hey-day of the kind that the church has not experienced since the anti-Modernist Pius popes. This catechism constantly talks of authority (above all of 'the church') and hardly ever of democracy. For the 'World Catechism' takes its place in a whole series of curial documents which show that Rome does not want freedom in plurality but only subjection to a single party line. Its very structure, with numbered paragraphs – the 'Roman-Catholic' faith has 2863 items in the year 1993 – recalls the *Codex Iuris Canonici*. What would our Lord Jesus Christ have said to this? However, an important function of this codex of faith, which weighs more than a kilo, will be not so much the 'edification' of the communities as the disciplining and regulating of bishops, pastors, teachers of religion and theologians.

Once again a great opportunity has been lost for the Catholic world church to hand on the universal Christian message to the many different cultures and nations of this earth in a really credible way. Given the plural world in which we live, at the end of the twentieth century a catechism of this kind is no longer an appropriate instrument for the proclamation of faith. What we urgently need is a basic and concentrated proclamation of the faith in keeping with the gospel, a proclamation which at the same time represents a true inculturation of the cause of Jesus Christ in the different peoples and cultures: a convincing translation of the original Christian message into today's time and world.

Hans Küng

The editors of the Special Column are Norbert Greinacher and Bas van Iersel. The content of the Special Column does not necessarily reflect the views of the Editorial Board of Concilium.

Contributors

SIDBE SEMPORÉ, a Dominican, was born in Ougadougou, Burkina-Faso, in 1938. He studied the Bible and theology in France, Austria, Israel and Switzerland and gained a diploma at the École Biblique in Jerusalem. He has taught and researched in Bible and theology at Bénin, in Nigeria and on the Ivory Coast. He has written articles and studies on the religious life, the African Christian churches, and other related topics. He is director of the journal *Pentecôte d'Afrique*.

Address: BP 479, Cotonou, République de Bénin, West Africa.

JOSÉ M. DE MESA was born in Manila in 1946, obtained his PhD in Religious Studies in 1978 at the Catholic University of Louvain and did post-doctoral studies at St Paul University in Ottawa, Canada, in 1986. He is Professor of Systematic Theology at the East Asian Pastoral Institute in the Philippines and is married with three children. He has written widely on inculturation, his field of special interest, in the context of lowland Filipino culture. Publications include *'And God Said, "Bahala Na!"': The Theme of Providence in the Lowland Filipino Context*; *In Solidarity with the Culture*; *Kapag Namayani Ang Kagandahang-loob ngg Diyos*; and, with a colleague, *Doing Theology* and *Doing Christology*. His most recent work is on 'Marriage as Discipleship'.

Address: East Asian Pastoral Institute, PO Box 221, 1101 UP Campus, QC, Philippines.

JAN RUIJTER was born in Wormer, North Holland, in 1940. He studied at the Hageveld Seminary in Warmond and in 1966 was ordained priest and appointed chaplain in Beverwijk. The Critical Community of Ijmond formed around him, and in 1968 he set up the Septuagint Movement of critical priests, preachers and laity. This movement has held congresses in many European countries and organized some 'shadow synods' in Rome. In connection with his church work he has also been involved in action relating to South Africa, Vietnam and Chile. In 1980 he was appointed Co-ordinator of the Moses House and the Moses and Aaron Church in

Amsterdam. The Moses House is a centre for adult education. It works for the aged, ethnic groups, the homeless, those with AIDS, and so on. Celebrations, exhibitions, demonstrations and concerts take place in the Moses and Aaron Church. Jan Ruijter has worked on many publications in connection with all these activities.

Address: Mozeshuis, Waterloopplein 205, 1011 PG Amsterdam, Netherlands.

ALBERT VILLARÓ was born in La Seu d'Urgell in 1964. He gained his licentiate in mediaeval history at the University of Barcelona and is now municipal archivist in La Seu d'Urgell, where he is working on his doctoral thesis on the perception of the landscape in the High Middle Ages. He has written *Causes i Conseqüències des despoblament*, MAB–6, Alt Pirineu 1989; *Els megàlits i la cultura popular de l'Alt Urgell*, 1989, and *Entre bosc i lo riu hi passave la vida*, both published by the Ministry of Culture; and *La ciutat i el riu*, Caixa de Catalunya 1992. Articles include 'La pesta negra, el 1348, a la Seu d'Urgell', *Urgellia* VIII, 1987; 'Noves dades sobre la pesta negra a la Seu (1348). Disposicions pietoses l'any de la pesta', *Urgellia* IX, 1988/9.

Address: Arxiu Municipal, 24700 La Seu d'Urgell, Lleida, Spain.

ANDRÉS TORRES QUIERUGA was born in Galicia in 1940. He studied at the Universidad de Comillas and gained doctorates in philosophy in the University of Santiago and in theology at the Gregorian. He is editor of *Encrucillada. Revista Galega de Pensamento Cristián*, and teaches philosophy of religion at the University of Santiago.

His books include: *Constitución y Evolución del Dogma*, Madrid 1977; *Recuperar la salvación*, Madrid 1979; *Nova aproximacion a unha filosofia da saudade*, Vigo 1981; *La revelación de Dios en la realización del hombre*, Madrid 1987; *Creo en Dios Padre*, Santander 1986; *Noción, religación, transcendencia*, Coruna 1990; *El cristianismo en el mundo de hoy*, Santander 1992; *El dialogo de las religiones*, Santander 1992. He has also written many articles.

Address: O. Curraliño, 23 G, 15705 Santiago, Spain.

MICHEL DENEKEN was born in Strasbourg in 1957 and studied German, literature and theology there. He was ordained priest in 1985 and teaches sociology in the Strasbourg Faculty of Catholic Theology. He is research-ing into the history of the concept of the church as a sacrament of salvation. Publications include *Le salut par le croix dans la théologie catholique contemporaine*, Paris 1986; *Une Eglise locale face au nazisme: l'Eglise d'Alsace, 1940–1945*, Strasbourg 1988.

Address: 136, route de Polygone, F 67100, Strasbourg, France.

WERNER JEANROND was born in Saarbrücken in 1955. He studied theology, philosophy and German at the universities of Saarbrücken, Regensburg and Chicago, and since 1981 has taught systematic theology at Trinity College, Dublin. He is a member of the editorial board of *Concilium*. His publications include *Text and Interpretation as Categories of Theological Thought*, Dublin and New York 1988, and *Theological Hermeneutics: Development and Significance*, London and New York 1991; with Jennifer L. Rike he has edited *Radical Pluralism and Truth: David Tracy and the Hermeneutics of Religion*, New York 1991.

Address: School of Biblical and Theological Studies, Trinity College, University of Dublin, Dublin 2, Ireland.

VIGAN GUROIAN is Associate Professor of Theology and Ethics at Loyola College in Baltimore, Maryland. He also serves as Director of Studies at St Nersess Armenian Seminary in New Rochelle, New York. He is the author of *Incarnate Love: Essays in Orthodox Ethics*, University of Notre Dame 1987. He has published numerous articles on the religious, political and moral dimensions of the Armenian genocide. He is now completing a new book, *Ethics after Christendom: Toward an Ecclesial Christian Ethics*, due to be published in 1993.

Address: Loyola College in Maryland, Baltimore, Maryland 21210 USA.

MARY E. HUNT PhD is a Catholic feminist theologian. She is co-founder and co-director of the Women's Alliance for Theology, Ethics and Ritual (WATER) in Silver Spring, Maryland, USA. She serves as co-chair of the Women and Religion Section of the American Academy of Religion and on the editorial board of the *Journal of Feminist Studies in Religion*. She lectures and writes widely on feminist ethics and is active in the women-church movement. Her recent publications include *Fierce Tenderness: A Feminist Theology of Friendship*, which merited the Crossroad Women's Studies Award for 1990, and the volume, *From Woman-Pain to Woman-Vision*, edited by Anne McGrew Bennett.

Address: Women's Alliance for Theology, Ethics and Ritual (WATER), 8035 13th Street, Silver Spring, Maryland 20910, USA.

RICHARD N. FRAGOMENI is Assistant Professor of Word and Worship at the Catholic Theological Union, Chicago. He holds masters degrees in liturgy and music, and a doctorate in sacramental studies. His articles have appeared in various journals and dictionaries, including *Pastoral Music*, *The New Theology Review*, and *The New Dictionary of Sacramental Worship*. He is co-editor of *A Promise of Presence: Essays in Honor of David N. Power*, 1992. He is a presbyter of the Diocese of Albany, New York.

Address: Catholic Theological Union, 5401 S. Cornell Avenue, Chicago, Ill. 60615–5698, USA.

DAVID N. POWER has been on the editorial board of *Concilium* since 1969 and has now retired from it. This is the last issue which he will edit. A native of Dublin, Ireland, he is currently Professor of Theology and Liturgy at The Catholic University of America, Washington, D C. His latest publication is *Eucharistic Mystery. Revitalizing the Tradition*, New York 1992.

Address: Catholic University of America, Dept of Theology, Washington DC 20064, USA.

Members of the Advisory Committee for Liturgy

Directors

Kabasele Lumbala	Mbuji Mayi	Zaire
David Power OML	Washington, DC	Zaire

Members

Ad Blijlevens CSSR	Heerlen	The Netherlands
Boris Bobrinskoy	Boulogne	France
Londi Boka di Mpasi SJ	Kinshasa-Gombe	Zaire
Anscar Chupungco OSB	Rome	Italy
Mary Collins OSB	Washington, DC	USA
Irenée-Henri Dalmais OP	Paris	France
Luigi Della Torre	Rome	Italy
Michel Dujarier	Ouidah	Bénin
Joseph Gelineau SJ	Moret sur Loing	France
Maucyr Gibin SSS	Sao Paulo, SP	Brazil
Kathleen Hughes RSCJ	Chicago, IL,	USA
Denis Hurley OMI	Durban	South Africa
Aidan Kavanagh OSB	New Haven, Conn.	USA
Guy Lapointe OP	Montreal	Canada
Juan Llopis	Barcelona	Spain
Gerard Lukken	Tilburg	The Netherlands
Luis Maldonado	Madrid	Spain
Paul Puthanangady SDB	Bangalore	India
Gail Ramshaw	Philadelphia, PA	USA
Heinrich Rennings	Paderborn	Germany
Philippe Rouillard OSB	Rome	Italy
Anton Scheer	Rosmalen	The Netherlands
Kevin Seasoltz OSB	Washington, DC	USA
Robert Taft SJ	Rome	Italy
Evangelista Vilanova OSB	Montserrat	Spain
Geoffrey Wainwright	Durham, NC	USA

Concilium

Issues of *Concilium* to be published in 1993

Messianism through History

edited by Wim Beuken, Sean Freyne and Anton Weiler

Explores the role that the notion of a Messiah has played in determining Jewish and Christian self-identities through history. After a first section on the latest understanding of the biblical background it traces messianic thought in Judaism and Christianity in the Middle Ages before discussing the implications of messianic belief today.

03018 8   1993/1   *February*

Any Room for Christ in Asia?

edited by Leonardo Boff and Virgil Elizondo in collaboration with Aloysius Pieris and Mary-John Mananzan

In Asia, Christians are a very small percentage of the people. Is this inevitable? A first section looks at the guises in which 'Christ' entered Asia and non-Christian perceptions of Christ; this is followed by accounts of specific current theological interpretations of Christ in Asian churches.

03019 6   1993/2   *April*

The Spectre of Mass Death

edited by David N. Power and F. Kabasele Lumbala

How does Christianity respond to catastrophes involving the sudden or mass death of thousands: war, famine and flood or epidemics like AIDS and drugs? This issue begins with examples of how people do in fact react, considers traditional responses to the question of evil in this connection, and then considers possible liturgical remembrance and forms of prayer.

03020 X   1993/3   *June*

Migrants and Refugees

edited by Dietmar Mieth and Lisa Sowle Cahill

The mass migration of people, especially in the Third World, as a result of war, famine or other pressures, is a major problem for the world. This issue offers accounts of what is actually happening on various continents, analyses the sociology of migration, considers the ethical issues and outlines possible Christian responses.

03022 6   1993/4   *August*

Reincarnation or Resurrection?

edited by Hermann Häring and Johann-Baptist Metz

A first part considers varieties of ideas of reincarnation in Hinduism, Buddhism, Latin American and African religion, and the popularity of reincarnation in modern belief; a second part adopts a similar approach to ideas of resurrection; the final part compares and contrasts the two approaches.

03021 8   1993/5   October

Mass Media

edited by John A. Coleman and Miklos Tomka

This issue recognizes that the media represent a complex phenomenon requiring deeper analysis than the church is often prepared to give. It seeks to help readers to understand better how the media work, how media communication should be 'read' and the moral and value issues involved in debates on the media.

03023 4   1993/6   December

Issues to be published in 1994

1994/1 Violence Against Women

1994/2 Christianity and Culture: A Mutual Enrichment

1994/3 Islam: A Challenge for Christianity

1994/4 Mysticism and the Institutional Crisis

1994/5 Catholic Identity

1994/6 Why Theology?

Concilium Subscription Information

Individual Annual Subscription (six issues): £30.00

Institution Annual Subscription (six issues): £40.00

Airmail subscriptions: add £10.00

Individual issues: £8.95 each

New subscribers please return this form:
for a two-year subscription, double the appropriate rate

(for individuals)   £30.00   (1/2 years)   . . . .

(for institutions)   £40.00   (1/2 years)   . . . .

Airmail postage
outside Europe +£10.00   (1/2 years)   . . . .

                        Total . . . .

I wish to subscribe for one/two years as an individual/institution
(delete as appropriate)

Name/Institution . . . .

Address . . . .

. . . .

. . . .

I enclose a cheque for . . . . payable to SCM Press Ltd

Please charge my Access/Visa/Mastercard no. . . . .

Signature . . . . .Expiry Date . . . .

Please return this form to:
SCM PRESS LTD 26-30 Tottenham Road, London N1 4BZ

Books available from Orbis Books

The Cosmotheandric Experience
Emerging Religious Consciousness
Raimon Panikkar
edited with an introduction by Scott Eastham

'The political implication of Panikkar's refiguration of the primordial unity of the worldly, the human and the Divine cannot be under-estimated. It beckons Wisdom as we abide in our time' (*Dr William F. Vendley*, World Conference on Religion and Peace).

The scholar who has lived and worked on the boundaries between West and East, Hinduism, Buddhism and Christianity; philosophy, science and theology describes the arrival of new ways of intuiting reality. The cosmotheandric experience denotes an essential inter-twining of the cosmic, the human and the divine - all interpenetrating dimensions of a single whole.

ISBN: 0 88344 862 9 cased   150pp index

Ecology and Justice Series
Healing Breath
Zen Spirituality for a Wounded Earth
Ruben L. F. Habito

Having earned a doctorate in Buddhist studies from the University of Tokyo, Habito has written widely on religion and socio-ecological issues. *Healing Breath* takes account of the Buddha's remark that it is fruitless to ask theoretical questions about the origins of a mortal ill-ness - what is important is tending to the sick. He locates the habits of mind and heart that wound persons and the environment, and points the way to developing instead those habits that will heal.

ISBN: 0 88344 919 6 paper   125pp index

Available from Orbis Books, Maryknoll NY 10545 USA